King's Head Theatre

T0127298

STRANGERS IN BETWEEN

BY TOMMY MURPHY

This production of *Strangers in Between* opened at the
King's Head Theatre, London, on 21 June 2016

The play was premiered by Griffin Theatre Company at the
SBW Stables Theatre, Sydney, on 11 February 2005

STRANGERS IN BETWEEN
BY TOMMY MURPHY

CAST

SHANE   Roly Botha
WILL/BEN   Dan Hunter
PETER   Stephen Connery-Brown

PRODUCTION TEAM

Director   Adam Spreadbury-Maher
Designer   Becky-Dee Trevenen
Lighting Designer   Richard Williamson
Sound Designer   Jon McLeod
Casting Director   Andrew Davies
Stage Manager   Christine Collins
Assistant Director   Jen Davis
Movement and   Lawrence Carmichael
Fight Director
Dialect Coach   Elspeth Morrison

THANKS

Simon Burke, Eren Celikdemir, Guy Edmonds, Edward Green,
Nick Hardcastle, Nicole Peters, Jenny Stow; Ben Hall, Charlie
Weedon and Lily Williams from Curtis Brown; Anthony Blair and
Jane Cameron from The Cameron Creswell Agency; Lizzie Hopkins.

CAST BIOGRAPHIES

Roly Botha – Shane
Strangers in Between is Roly's professional theatre debut, following a course of study at the National Youth Theatre of Great Britain (Epic Stages, 2015) and Identity School of Acting (Advanced Acting, 2016). Roly would like to thank Phil King and Neil Hornsby for their advice and guidance.

Dan Hunter – Will/Ben
Hailing from the Australian coastal town of Port Macquarie, Dan grew up enjoying all the opportunities a sun-soaked lifestyle had on offer; incidentally this did not include many chances to tread the boards. After moving to Sydney in 2006, Dan's passion for performance began to flourish with study at Actors Centre Australia (ACA) and later the Australian Academy of Dramatic Art (AADA). Dan's most noted work in Sydney includes *A Masked Ball* (La Fura dels Baus & Opera Australia for the 2013 Sydney Festival); *Rocket Man* (Subtlenuance); *Seven Jewish Children* (Splinter Theatre Company); *Great Expectations* (bAKEHOUSE Theatre Company); *Ben Hur* (Stadefrance); *Metamorphoses* (Apocolypse & bAKEHOUSE Theatre Companies); *Trocadero Dance Palace* (Sydney Festival 2011); *The Real Story* (Short+Sweet Gala Final 2011) and *Showtrain* (New Musicals Aust.). Recent starring roles include *Humanity on the Edge* (Roughcast Collective); short films *Hot Seat* (Anna Mimi Jayson) and *The Window Cleaner* (Dan Eycott) both currently doing the festival circuit, as well as the comedy web-series *The Adventures of Ozzie and Scott* (Oliver Brown).

Stephen Connery-Brown – Peter
Stephen trained at East15 Acting School and graduated in 2006. This is Stephen's second Australian play in a row having played Dad in *The Sum of Us* for Above the Stag, at Vauxhall late last year. Prior to that he played Malvolio in The Malachite's summer tour of *Twelfth Night* – having previously performed as Gloucester in *King Lear*, York in *Richard II*, and Shylock in *The Merchant of Venice* for the same company. Stephen has also completed a season at Park Theatre last year – of the UK premiere of *The Glass Protégé*. Other work includes commercials, short films, corporate videos, theatre-in-education and radio.

PRODUCTION TEAM BIOGRAPHIES

Tommy Murphy – Author

Tommy is an award-winning playwright, television and film writer. *Holding the Man*, Tommy's incredibly successful adaptation for the stage, has been produced across the world and continues to be a huge hit in Australia. His feature film adaptation for *Holding the Man*, for which he was also Associate Producer, was the gala presentation at the 2016 BFI Flare Festival. It stars Anthony LaPaglia, Ryan Corr, Guy Pearce and Kerry Fox and has already won the Australian Writers' Guild Award and the Film Critics' Circle of Australia Award for Best Screenplay. The play won multiple awards including the NSW Premier's Literary Award, the Australian Writers' Guild Award and the Philip Parsons Award. Tommy's play *Gwen in Purgatory* won the WA Premier's Award and the prestigious Richard Burton Prize. Tommy has written for the highly acclaimed Australian TV drama *Devil's Playground* (winner Logie Most Outstanding Miniseries or Telemovie and AACTA Best Telefeature or Mini Series) and is working on various original television projects. His new stage works include *The Desirables* for the state theatre company of Western Australia and a new play for Sydney's Belvoir Theatre. Murphy's adaptation of Lorca's *Blood Wedding* formed part of the London 2012 Cultural Olympiad. Other plays include *Troy's House* and *Strangers in Between* (NSW Premier's Literary Award Winner). He is a Creative Fellow at the University of Queensland.

Adam Spreadbury-Maher – Director

Adam is an award-winning director and producer. He is the founding Artistic Director of the Cock Tavern Theatre, OperaUpClose and the Hope Theatre. In 2009 he produced *La bohème* at the Cock Tavern and Soho Theatres, winner of the Olivier Award for Best Opera. Directing highlights: *Trainspotting* (King's Head/UK tour); *A Tale of Two Cities* adapted by Terence Rattigan and John Gielgud (King's Head/Australia); *Dead Party Animals* (Hope); Louis Nowra's *Cosi* and Daniel Reitz's *Studies for a Portrait* (White Bear); Peter Gill's *The York Realist* and *The Sleepers' Den* (Riverside Studios); Hannie Rayson's *Hotel Sorrento* and a new play by Edward Bond, *There Will Be More* (Cock Tavern); and in Australia Jonathan Harvey's *Beautiful Thing* and Joe Orton's *Loot*. For OperaUpClose he directed *Tosca* (West End/King's Head/UK and Sweden national tour), *Ballo* (A Masked Ball) and *Madam Butterfly* (King's Head). Producing highlights: Jack Hibberd's *A Stretch of the Imagination*, the hit musical *Pins and Needles*, and the landmark six-play Edward Bond retrospective (Cock Tavern); *The Coronation of Poppea*, *Shock Treatment* and *Someone to Blame* (King's Head); and *Don Giovanni* (Soho). In 2010 Adam became Artistic Director of the King's Head and won Best Artistic Director in the Fringe Report Awards. In 2011 he was nominated for Best Director in the Off-West End Awards. Find Adam on Twitter @ASMchats

Becky-Dee Trevenen – Designer

Becky-Dee is a costume and set designer based in London. Whilst completing a Bachelor of Dramatic Art (Design) at the National Institute of Dramatic Art (NIDA) in Sydney, she developed an interest in collaborative theatre-making, site-specific, immersive and devised work. Upon graduating, she worked alongside director Baz Luhrmann as concept artist and visual researcher for *Chanel No.5 – The One That I Want – The Film*, as well as designing numerous film and theatre productions. Becky-Dee is passionate about developing and realising new work and has designed many world premiere productions in the last year, most notably *Miss Sarah* by Ella Cook (dir. Angus Wilkinson, Cicada Studios); *Crooks* (Colab); and *Russian Dolls*

(King's Head). On top of this, Becky-Dee works frequently as a design assistant for immersive theatre company Punchdrunk. Her credits include the Punchdrunk Enrichment productions: *Against Captains' Orders* and *The Lost Lending Library*.

Richard Williamson – Lighting Designer

Trained at LAMDA, previous work includes: *Richard III, An Arab Tragedy* (Swan Theatre Stratford/international tour); *Septimus Bean* (Unicorn); *Shrapnel, Mare Rider, Boy With a Suitcase, Peer Gynt, Macbeth, A Midsummer Night's Dream, The Night Just Before the Forest, Tartuffe, Through a Cloud, King Arthur, Mojo Mickybo, The Great Theatre of the World, Tombstone Tales, The Country* (Arcola); *The Easter Rising and Thereafter* (Jermyn Street); *Rotterdam* (Theatre503); *The Dark Side of Love* (Roundhouse); *In My Name, Boris World King* (Trafalgar Studios); *Amphibians* (Bridewell); *Thrill Me* (Tristan Bates/Charing Cross Theatre/UK tour); *The Last Session* (Tristan Bates); *Twentieth Century Boy* (New Wolsey, Ipswich); *Play Size* (Young Vic); *The Al-Hamlet Summit* (Tokyo International Festival/international tour); *Best Friends* (New End); *Crossing the Line* (Baltimore College, USA); *Onysos the Wild* (Theatre503/Traverse Edinburgh); *Ballo, Tosco, Denial, Someone to Blame* (King's Head); *Summer Begins* (Southwark Playhouse). Richard is Head of Production for C venues at the Edinburgh Festival, and is a Trustee of the King's Head Theatre.

Jon McLeod – Sound Designer

Jon studied BA Sound Design at the Leeds College of Music and MA Advanced Theatre Practice at the Central School of Speech and Drama. Recent credits include *Tribute Acts, Ross & Rachel, Penguinpig, Lost in the Neuron Forest, A Conversation, The Fanny Hill Project* (UK tour); *Tether, Much Further Out Than You Thought* (Underbelly); *Heartbreak Hotel* (The Jetty); *Spine* (Soho); *Macbeth, Followers* (Southwark Playhouse); *Arthur's World* (Bush); *Free Fall* (The Pleasance); *Stink Foot* (The Yard); *The Boy in Darkness, Nightmare Dreamer, Flying Roast Goose* (Blue Elephant); *People Show #131* (Putney Library); *Party Skills for the End of the World, 66 Minutes in Damascus* (Shoreditch Town Hall); *The Eyes Have It* (Imagine Watford); *Borderline Vultures* (The Lowry) and *Organs of Little Apparent Importance* (HighTide Festival).

Andrew Davies – Casting Director

King's Head casting: *I Went To A Fabulous Party..., F*cking Men, Nobody's Business, 5 Guys Chillin', Cosi, Russian Dolls, Spitting Image*. Other casting: *Mockingbird* (Biscroca); *Nation Down* (Barreto); *All's Well That Ends Well, She Stoops to Conquer* (Changeling); *Christie in Love* (Rough Haired Pointer); *Choice* (Vernal Media); *An Old Man of the Hills* (Dryades).

Christine Collins – Stage Manager

Christine graduated with a BA Hons in Drama from Queen's University Belfast before undertaking further training at Edinburgh Lighting, Sound and Stage Management School. She has had the pleasure of working with companies such as National Theatre of Scotland, A Moment's Peace, Lung Ha Theatre and Bard in the Botanics before undertaking her new role as Resident Stage Manager at King's Head Theatre.

Jen Davis – Assistant Director

Jen is a Trainee Resident Director at the King's Head Theatre. She graduated from the University of Birmingham in 2013, after reading Drama and Theatre Arts. Since then she has directed fifteen short plays for a number of new-writing festivals (including nights at the Birmingham REP, New Wimbledon Studio, LOST Theatre and Old Joint Stock Theatre). Jen was a Director on the Birmingham Repertory Theatre's artist development programme: Foundry (2014–2015) and showcased work at their monthly scratch nights. She also directed *Billy* for the REP's Home Theatre Project. In 2014, she co-founded and produced 'Shoot Festival', a new platform for emerging artists making work in Coventry, which made a return to the Shop Front Theatre in March 2016. She was the Associate Producer on Rough Haired Pointer's production of *Christie in Love*. Assistant Directing credits include *Russian Dolls* and *Trainspotting* (King's Head). She is also an assistant producer for Sixteenfeet Productions; a site-specific theatre company based in Brixton.

Lawrence Carmichael – Movement and Fight Director

Lawrence Carmichael is an actor, singer, fight director and movement specialist with over twenty years' experience in stage combat and physical theatre. In Australia he has worked regularly with most major companies including Sydney Theatre Company, Opera Australia, Company B, NIDA, Bell Shakespeare & ABC TV. Qualified by both the BADC & SAFDi, he continues as a fight and movement specialist in the UK. Previous work in the UK includes *King Lear*, *Woyzeck*, *Lot & His Wife*, six Edward Bond plays, *Madam Butterfly*, *Don Giovanni*, as well as battle scenes for MBC Television in Morocco and the feature film *Cockneys Vs Zombies*. Lawrence has notably appeared the UK tour of *South Pacific* and in Tommy Murphy's other London triumph, *Holding the Man* at Trafalgar Studios. He is very excited to be bringing more of Tommy's work to the London stage. www.lawrencecarmichael.com

Elspeth Morrison – Dialect Coach

Elspeth Morrison is a renowned voice coach. She's thrilled to continue her long association with the King's Head and works for many theatres including the Bush, Hampstead, and the National Theatre. She also works for BBC Comedy and the BBC Radio Drama Company. When not coaching accents she helps broadcasters and presenters for the BBC, ITV and Sky. She has also made numerous guest appearances on talk shows on the subject of voice.

A Note from the Artistic Director of the King's Head Theatre

Hello,

I'm thrilled to present the European premiere of Tommy Murphy's *Strangers in Between*.

Whilst the the themes and setting are very close to my heart, Murphy's acute portrait of a sixteen-year-old boy adrift in a world of possibilities, straddling adulthood and childhood in equal measure encompasses an experience we can all relate to. Growing up.

Remarkably, *Strangers in Between* has never been staged in Europe, but was a critical and commercial hit in Australia, going on to win the prestigious New South Wales Premier's Literary Award for Best Play. I'm delighted that our audiences will have the opportunity to see such highly regarded writing from Down Under.

If you are a regular to the King's Head I would like to welcome you back – and if it is your first time here, where have you been hiding? In either case, I really hope you enjoy your stay, and that we see you again soon.

It is vital that we keep producing theatre of significance and strive for the highest artistic excellence as possible. We are unfunded and rely completely on the box office (thanks for buying a ticket) and from donations from individuals. If you fancy, please do consider dropping a few coins in the bucket on the way out. We pay a rather high rent to be here, and unfortunately take no revenue from the bar. If you come here often, you could consider formalising our relationship by becoming a friend of the King's Head. Your support means that we will be here next time you visit, and as the oldest surviving pub theatre in London, that is something we really care about. Thanks again for coming, enjoy your stay and we hope to see you again soon.

Adam

Adam Spreadbury-Maher
King's Head Theatre – Artistic Director

King's Head Theatre

WORK IN OUR COMMUNITY

We work with a number of charities and organisations both locally and further afield on a regular basis. Our friends in the community include:

BARNET COLLEGE JOB COACHES
CRI ISLINGTON
ISLINGTON COMMUNITY THEATRE
ISLINGTON GIVING
JEWISH CARE
MOUSETRAP THEATRE PROJECTS
SAFEHANDS FOR MOTHERS
SINGLE HOMELESS PEOPLE
VOLUNTARY ACTION ISLINGTON
NSPCC ISLINGTON
POSITIVE EAST
CRISIS

If you're involved with a charity and want to find out more about how you can work with the King's Head Theatre contact Rachel Illingworth via rachel.illingworth@kingsheadtheatre.com or 020 7226 8561.

A Brief History of the King's Head Theatre Building

The King's Head Theatre stands on a plot of land that has been used as a public house since 1543, though for most of its history it has been known as the King's Head Tavern (the name itself coming from an old story about Henry VIII supposedly stopping for a pint on his way to see his mistress). The current building dates back to the 1800s.

Dan Crawford took over the venue in 1970, and founded the King's Head Theatre in a room that had been used as a boxing ring and pool hall, establishing the first pub theatre in London since Shakespeare's day. Under his leadership the pub became well-known for ringing up pounds, shillings and pence until 2008, a full thirty-seven years after the rest of the UK had switched to decimal currency. The pub is packed full of other period details, including gas lights, the original bar, old photography, and coal fires that burn continuously throughout the winter.

Crawford led the venue for thirty-five years, establishing it as a breeding ground for new talent and great work. The walls of the pub display the multitude of famous faces that began their career here. In 2010, Olivier Award-winning UpClose Productions became the theatre's resident company, and Adam Spreadbury-Maher was appointed the venue's second Artistic Director, working alongside Robin Norton-Hale who led the company's opera programme.

At the start of 2015 the third chapter of the King's Head Theatre began as the Theatre celebrated her 45th anniversary. With the departure of OperaUpClose, Artistic Director Adam Spreadbury-Maher chose to stay on, refocusing the venue's artistic policy towards new work and critical theatrical revivals. High quality and accessible classical music remains a part of the programme with Charles Court Opera joining the venue as an associate company. This year the King's Head will present twelve main-stage productions including the first UK revival of Colin Spencer's *Spitting Image* and following the recent success of *Cosi fan Tutte* we are please to be presenting an exciting new version of Puccini's *La bohème*. We certainly aren't slowing down!

The venue's reputation for nurturing new talent continues, with pioneering Trainee Director scheme (winner of the Royal Anniversary Trust Award in 1992) still being run by the King's Head Theatre. Recent graduates have gone on to work at the National Theatre, RSC, Lyric Hammersmith and the Globe, plus many other internationally-renowned companies.

The building is continually evolving. Recent additions to the theatre include the introduction of allocated seating, new house lights in the auditorium and air conditioning, with many more improvements planned in the future. See you again soon?

www.equity.org.uk

The King's Head Theatre is delighted to be working with Equity, the UK's largest trade union for the performing arts.

We are proud to be one of the very few small-scale unfunded theatres in the UK to have an Equity House Agreement.

The Agreement states that we will pay all performers and stage managers in King's Head Theatre productions an Equity-approved rate for rehearsals and performances, which complies with all legal requirements relating to National Insurance, holiday pay and National Living Wage. This is not the same as the Equity rates for subsidised or West End theatres, as Equity recognise that these rates were not intended to be applied to a 118-seat, unfunded theatre such as ours. It is a unique agreement which recognises and formalises our commitment to paying artists and stage managers a fair wage for the work that they do.

'The King's Head is leading the way for fringe theatre in acknowledging that they not only have a legal responsibility to pay the National Living Wage and respect other workers' rights, but also that the industry expects them to work with artists through their union, Equity. Our agreement with the King's Head (now in its sixth year) is a substantial beginning to improving the working lives of artists at the King's Head and has put us solidly on the way to creating a fairer fringe.'

Paul W Fleming
London Area Theatre Organiser; Equity

King's Head Theatre Staff

COME HERE OFTEN?

If you like the work we're doing here at the King's Head Theatre, perhaps you'd like to support us by becoming a Friend or Patron of the Theatre.

We are a completely unfunded producing house and so we rely on box office sales and kind donations from members of the public who share our artistic vision and believe in what we're doing.

If you would like to join us and help us continue to produce high-quality work at affordable prices, there are a number of ways to do so:

Become a Friend £25 per year
Priority booking in advance of the general public
Receive our King's Head Friends' newsletter

Key to the Stage Door £150 per year
All of the above, plus:
Acknowledgment in programmes
Invitations to patrons' events

Key to the Dressing Room £500 per year
All of the above, plus:
Free upgrade to 'premium' reserved seats at any performance
Free programmes for any production upon request

Key to the King's Head £1,000 per year
All of the above, plus:
Drinks with the creative team

To discuss becoming a Friend please contact Oscar French on
oscar@kingsheadtheatre.com or call **020 7226 8561**

King's Head Theatre Friends

We are only able to carry on producing work of the quality we strive for through fundraising activities, our patrons and sponsors, and by selling tickets through our box office. Our patrons and sponsors support us with a range of valuable contributions which allow us to continue our work, acquire particular assets we need and to fund productions.

PATRONS

Inger Almström, Richard Buxton & Sarah Redhead, Gareth Cadwallader and Nancy Neville, David Crook, David Lacey and Abigail Day, Conrad Freedman, John Ward, Dr Lois Potter, Paul Thomson and Paul Vaight.

FRIENDS

Mark Annear, Mary & Dave Aspinall, Nick Baldwin, Michael Baptista, Liz Barnes, Annie Barker, Professor Bernard Barker, Graham Barnes, Louisa Bell, Nick Bennett-Britton, Timothy & Nathalie Bibbs, Lucy Bradlow, Susie Bur-rows, Clare Burton, Tony & Jackie Burton, Ian Carson, Yiannis Chronakis, Nathan Coffey, Jeff Cloke, Richard Cole-man, Jeanette Collins, Robert Collinge, Martin Collins, Tony Cox, Edward Darby, Rachel Darwazeh, Terence Davis, Jonathan & Natalya de Lance-Holmes, Wouter Denhaan, Anthony Depledge, Elizabeth Devenish, Martin Donnelly, Cathy Donohue, Andrew Doyle, Richard & Carolyn Edmunds, Carole Ann Farquharson, Chris Finch, Gail Fitzgerald, Oliver Ford, Alison Foster, Lynne Freeman, Dale Franzen, Lynda Fry, Nicola Garcia, Hemda Garelick, Susan Gaskell, Jeff Gilbert, Nicola Gooch, Jonathan Green, Kevin Gwilt & Pat Trotter, Gareth Hadley, Richard Hale, Andrew Halsall, Anne Halsall, John Halsey, Dr Robert Hancock, Rachael Henry, Andrew Hochhauser, Deborah A. Holt, Kate Horn, Diana Hornsby, Margaret Howat, Joyce & Ben Hytner, Anne Ireland, David Kaskel, William Kessler, Jenny & Stephen Kingsley, Jan Knight, James Laing, Richard Laing, Martin Ledigo, Christopher & Judy Legge, Tim Levett, Jonathan Levy, Marina Lewycka, Morris Lipson & C. Poiriev, Susan Loppert, Alison Lurie, Nicola Manby, Graham Marchant, Ines Mareschal-Leduc, Jo Marsden, Sarah Matthias, Jeremy McCallum & Lynette Rees, Stephen Machin, Matthew Maxwell, Becky McAlees & Chris Johnston, Liz Meek, Richard Middleton, Rosie Millard, Daniel Monk, Michael Morrison, John & Janet Murphy, Janie New, Jeraine Olson, Caroline Orr, Margaret Orrell, Bob Osborne, Svetlana Paterson, David Peace, Leonard Peter, Fiona Piper, Eve Pleming, Nigel Pleming, Thane Prince, Beatrice Randall, Robert Read, Jenifer Reed, Gaynor Reynolds, Martin Reynolds, Chris Richardson-Child, Mary Robertson, Sue Robertson, Dr. Chris Rogers, Kate Rossini, Michael, Rubenstein, Ros Schwartz & Andrew Cowan, James Scott, Anouche Sherman, John & Margaret Skerritt, Christopher Smith, Dina & Martin Smith, Heather Smith & David Wilson, Huw Smith, David Stanford, John Tagholm, Chris Thompson, Lucy Turnbill, Ken & Sandy Tyrrell, Cathryn Vanderspar, Xavier Villers, Richard Wallace-Reid, Kate Wark, Mark Warwick, Jude Wheway & Peter Shakesby, Janet & Martyn Wilson, Emmeline & James Winterbotham, Paul Wyman, Rev Dennis Mihill, Gwen Kirstein, Margo Griffin-Wilson, Mr C J P Lindon, Mr T C Mitchell, Mary-Ann Tarver, Graham Taylor, Kirstein Hardie, Stephanie Freeman, Roy Batchelor, Kathleen Wets, Jennifer Brophy, Ellie Kayne, John Watson & Janis Higgins, Rollo Millership, Belton Flournoy, Ivor Cole, Lisa Werth, William McGuire, Swithin Fry, Stephen Claypole, Derek Stanley-Honnor, Emile Boustani, Susan Claris, Dr David Thame, Bridget Somekh, Kate Tonizzo, Nick Baldwin, Christopher, Regan Koch, Kallie Brenton, Mark Smith, Mr Scott Elliott, James Desmond-Caffrey, Martin Halfhide & George Acquah-Hayford, Paul Thomson, Victoria Maltby, Michael Beasley, Stephen Lumby, Sarah Bates, Geoffrey Weill, Charles Hicks, Jeffrey Fuller, Brian Smith, Mike Sharman, Christopher Raper, Alison Buck, Mr Calum Maclean, Diana King, Christopher Shadforth, Ant Babajee, Gerard Cabral, Anthony Thwaites, Jop Bekink, Jocelyn Cheek, Helen Tydeman, Patrick McDowell, Stephen Allen-Tidy, Linton Street, Anthony William Clough, James P Baker, Bert Aerts, Stephan Seissl, Cheryl Silverberg, Andrea Greystoke, Vanessa Yreeswijk-Van Mildert, Rebecca Crookshank, Sonia Porter, Paul Stevens, Coby Walter, Sam Butler, Kenneth Tyrell, Magnus Foss and Stuart Dickson.

STRANGERS IN BETWEEN

Tommy Murphy

For Hugh

Strangers in Between was first produced by the Griffin Theatre Company at the SBW Stables Theatre, Sydney, on 11 February 2005, with the following cast:

SHANE	Sam Dunn
WILL/BEN	Brett Stiller
PETER	Anthony Phelan
Director	David Berthold
Designer	Alice Babidge
Lighting Designer	Anthony Pearson

4

Characters

SHANE, *sixteen, but may appear older*
WILL, *early twenties*
PETER, *mid-fifties to mid-sixties*
BEN, *early twenties, Shane's brother*

The action takes place over several months in Sydney's Kings Cross in the early 2000s.

Note on Casting

The same actor plays both Will and Ben.

Shane's physical description of Will on pages 42-45 is part fantasy.

ACT ONE

A bottlo on the strip. SHANE *is at work.* WILL *is a customer choosing alcohol to buy.*

SHANE. Sorry.

WILL. What?

SHANE. I wasn't staring.

WILL. Okay.

SHANE. You look like someone.

WILL. Right.

SHANE. Sorry. Yeah. Do you need a hand?

WILL. Nah, just grabbing some grog.

SHANE. Let me know if you need a hand.

WILL. Thanks.

　　WILL *surveys the drinks.*

SHANE. What type of grog do you like?

WILL. All of it.

SHANE. Well, maybe you should get a selection.

WILL. Oh no. I'll just get this.

　　WILL *selects some pre-mixed bottles.*

SHANE. Good choice. Let me take that to the register for you.

WILL. I'm right.

SHANE. Cool. This way. Um. Okay. 'Vodka Black Ice.' I think there's a button for that. Six-pack?

WILL. Four-pack.

SHANE. Four-pack of Vodka Black Ice. No. I can't see the button for it.

WILL. Maybe you scan it.

SHANE. No. No I think there's a button. Do you know how much it is?

WILL. About seven or eight bucks.

SHANE. Is it?

WILL. Nup. Let me check.

SHANE. Oh no. I'll check. I have to learn the prices. It's twelve ninety-five.

WILL. Cool.

SHANE. Twelve ninety-five? Is that a rip-off?

WILL. No. I mean they're like six-fifty each in a bar.

SHANE. Really? Sounds like a rip-off to me. Okay. Twelve ninety-five.

SHANE *examines the cash register.*

Oh, how does this thing work?

WILL. They usually scan it.

SHANE. Oh, have you been here before?

WILL. Yeah, heaps.

SHANE. Oh okay. Let's see. I thought I typed in the prices or something.

SHANE *scans the drinks.*

Oh yeah, no, that's right. It must be the wines I have a button for. You'd think there'd be a button for these too because buttons are easier, hey.

WILL. Yeah.

SHANE *is waiting for the register to open.*

SHANE. I might practise scanning stuff later.

WILL. Cool.

SHANE. Ooh, hang on. I'd have to clear each sale, wouldn't I?

WILL. I wouldn't know.

SHANE. Yeah. Now it hasn't opened. I thought the register just opened when you scan it.

WILL. I want to pay with EFTPOS anyway.

SHANE. Oh Jesus. You haven't got cash?

WILL. Just shrapnel.

SHANE. The manager will be back soon. Do you mind waiting a second?

WILL. I kind of have to go.

SHANE. Oh, okay. I don't know how to open the register, that's all. Why did he, ohhh. I mean, why did he leave me here? I can't do this. I've been here one day. This isn't even my shirt. My name's not Michelle.

SHANE*'s shirt is embroidered with the name 'Michelle'.*

I mean this is... look I'm really sorry. Err.

SHANE *checks his pockets.*

I don't have... how much is it? Yeah see I don't have any change in my pocket.

WILL. Oh, that's okay. I'll just wait.

SHANE. He won't be long.

WILL. Cool.

SHANE. Sorry, hey.

WILL. So you've just started here?

SHANE. Yeah. Yesterday. I worked next door before that.

WILL. Maccas?

SHANE. Yeah. Just for a week.

WILL. Right. And is it good here?

SHANE. Well, yeah, I think so. Um, some of the guys are arseholes. The manager's a bit of a cock. He just thinks I'm so dumb.

PETER *enters*.

WILL. Is this him?

SHANE. No. I don't know who this is. (*To* PETER.) Evening. Do you need a hand?

PETER. Oh well, that's good service. Just looking for a wine.

SHANE. Can I help you?

PETER. Oh yes, well, I think so. Just in the market for a reasonable Chardonnay, I think.

SHANE. Red or white?

PETER. Let's try white.

SHANE. Okay then.

PETER. Keep it cheap and cheerful. Just off to a family thing.

SHANE. These are our whites here.

PETER. Good. So what do you recommend?

SHANE. Oh, yeah. They're all good.

PETER. Mmmh, yes, no need for it to be good per se. It's not like they'll know, bless them.

SHANE. That looks cheap.

PETER. Perhaps cheaper I think. Although, I like that drop. I'll grab that one for my brother-in-law and me. Now, for my sister… Do you have Queen Adelaide?

SHANE. Um. I don't know.

PETER. Could get her a cask.

SHANE. There. There's Queen Adelaide.

PETER. Well spotted.

SHANE. Cool.

> PETER *selects a bottle.*

PETER. And how are you boys tonight?

SHANE. Good.

PETER. It's a lovely evening.

SHANE. Yeah.

PETER. Just gorgeous.

SHANE. How much for those? Do they say on them?

PETER. Thirteen ninety-five and six fifty.

SHANE. Okay. Nineteen dollars forty-five...

WILL. Twenty.

SHANE. No. Yes. Twenty forty-five, thanks.

PETER. Bargain. Thank you.

> PETER *hands over a twenty and a five-dollar note.*

SHANE. You don't have the exact?

PETER. Sorry.

> WILL *retrieves the change in his pocket.*

SHANE. Okay...

WILL. Hang on. (*To* PETER.) Here you are. There's four dollars and, hang on, fifty-five cents.

PETER. Thanking you.

WILL (*to* SHANE). You can pay me back when the register's opened.

SHANE. Oh, okay.

PETER. Cheerio, boys.

> PETER *leaves* WILL'*s money as a tip.*

SHANE. Bye, have a nice day, night.

PETER *exits*.

WILL. Yuck, old sleaze.

SHANE. What do you mean?

WILL. See how he looked at us?

SHANE. No.

WILL. Yeah, so gross. As if.

SHANE. Yeah.

WILL. I'm never going to be like that. And all that stuff about their families: get over it.

SHANE. Yeah.

WILL. So, are you going out after this?

SHANE. Oh I don't know. Probably not.

WILL. Oh right.

SHANE. You?

WILL. Yeah, I might. I mean, yeah, no, I definitely am. I'm just going to dinner at my friends' and then yeah, we're going out to get trashed.

SHANE. Where's good to go around here?

WILL. Are you from out of town?

SHANE. I've just moved here from Goulburn.

WILL. Oh right. Do you like it here?

SHANE. It's better than Goulburn.

WILL. What's wrong with Goulburn?

SHANE. I had to get out. It's better here. It's just better not knowing people. Everyone thinks they know everything about everyone in Goulburn.

WILL. Yeah. No Big Banana here but. That's what you've got, isn't it?

SHANE. A Big Merino actually. You've got a big Coke sign but. That's good.

WILL. Yeah guess so. And there's stuff to do in Sydney which is also good, I guess. Still must be fun to live in the country with all those… actually, no it would suck. It's good you moved. Better than hanging out there and hanging yourself or whatever young guys do there. Do you need someone to show you around?

SHANE. Yeah. Cool.

WILL. So what time do you finish?

SHANE. I finish in like half an hour but I can't tonight. I've gotta wait to get paid.

WILL. Oh well, maybe later in the week.

SHANE. Excellent, yeah.

WILL. Do you have a phone number?

SHANE. We have one here. I don't know what it is but. You could look it up or just come and see me. I'm working three hours every night this week except tomorrow. I usually start at five.

WILL. Okay then. I'll pop in.

SHANE. Cool. You're not a backpacker murderer or anything are you?

WILL. Hey? Um, are you a backpacker?

SHANE. No. No I mean you're not dodgy?

WILL. No.

SHANE. I know you're not. I could tell as soon as you came in. You've gotta be alert but. There's no alarm here. Some people try to steal stuff. I can tell. I'm just going to let them but. They might have needles.

WILL. Yeah. But you'll be all right.

SHANE. Do you wanna just take these? Make it cost the nine dollars and fifty-five cents that you gave that gross guy. I'll make it work out when the manager comes back.

WILL. You sure?

SHANE. He's probably just smoking pot out the back. He'll be stoned. It's fine.

WILL. Cool. Thanks heaps.

SHANE. Yeah.

WILL. Cool. Bye, Michelle.

SHANE. Yeah, nah, it's Shane.

WILL. I'm Will.

SHANE. Cool. Bye, Will.

WILL. Bye.

***

The Bourbon and Beefsteak. A week later.

SHANE *finds a table. He has a plate of oily nibblies in front of him; a spring roll, a cocktail frankfurt, some corn chips and a mini meat pie.* PETER *is nearby at another table.*

SHANE. Excuse me. Do you know how much longer they have the free bar snacks out for?

PETER. Just for happy hour.

SHANE. How long's that for?

PETER. Another hour and a half.

SHANE. Cool. You go to my bottlo, hey.

PETER. Oh, do I? Which one is that?

SHANE. The one next to Maccas.

PETER. Oh yes. You served me last week. I remember. The register was on the blink.

SHANE. Yeah. That's right. You got the Queen Adelaide.

PETER. I don't think so.

SHANE. Yeah, I'm learning all the names of them.

PETER. Good, I would have got the Rosemount. Hang on, no, I bought something nasty for my sister. She hated that.

SHANE. Oh right. Yeah, the Rosemount's cheap too. But not actually cheap. They're all expensive. Wine's just pricey.

PETER *drinks*.

I've never been here before. This is good, hey. Do you know how much the beefsteak is?

PETER. There's a menu there.

SHANE. Cool.

SHANE *holds up a Bourbon and Beefsteak menu*.

I might sit at your table.

PETER. I'm waiting for –

SHANE *sits at* PETER*'s table*.

SHANE. I like this place.

PETER. Yes. It's good.

Silence.

We call it 'the office'.

SHANE. What?

PETER. This place. My friend Graeme and I call it 'the office'. We're forever saying, 'I'll meet you at the office.' He's meant to be here now but he's held up at some hellish godchild's birthday party. He wanted moral support but I said, 'Pass the bloody parcel, I don't think so. I simply can't pull myself away from the office.' Was very funny.

SHANE. Oh right. (*Finishing reading the menu*.) Man! As if you'd order any of that when they give you free stuff.

PETER. Right, well, I think they want you to order a drink too.

SHANE. What a 'bourbon'? I got a glass of water.

PETER. Goodo.

SHANE. So do you live around here?

PETER. Yes.

SHANE. Yeah it's dodgy hey.

PETER. I've never had any trouble.

SHANE. Really? A girl got acid thrown on her face just near my house.

PETER. Isn't that dreadful?

SHANE. Yeah. Probably drug-related.

PETER. Maybe.

SHANE. Yeah. Do you want me to get you a plate of snacks?

PETER. Oh no. I'm fine. Yes, I quite like living amongst all this. I walk home past the prostitutes and the bikies and the junkies and somehow I feel at home.

SHANE. So what do you do?

PETER. Oh, I work for the government.

SHANE. As a what?

PETER. In one of their departments. Roads – main roads. I'm the head trainer in HR. It's all a bit boring. But I draw. That's my interesting side.

SHANE. Awesome. What do you draw?

PETER. Still life.

SHANE. Nude people.

PETER. No pots and domestic things.

SHANE. Cool. I did art at school.

PETER. Oh yeah.

SHANE. Yeah, but the teacher sucked and it was a bludge.

PETER. Oh well.

SHANE. Hey, can I ask you something?

PETER. I think so.

SHANE. Are you meant to keep honey in the fridge?

PETER. Oh.

SHANE. That's just something I've needed to ask someone.

PETER. No, you don't have to. It goes hard if you do.

SHANE. Oh. Yeah, I'm keeping it on a shelf – on a little
    bookshelf – but I didn't know if you're meant to or not.
    I won't put it in the fridge.

PETER. No, it's hard to spread.

SHANE. Yeah, as long as it won't go off.

PETER. No.

SHANE. Good. I don't have a fridge and I love honey. What
    about fabric softener?

PETER. On a shelf is fine.

SHANE. But do you have to use it?

PETER. No.

SHANE. Right. But if you do use it, do you have to use laundry
    powder as well?

PETER. Oh yes. It won't clean your clothes. It will just soften
    them.

SHANE. I thought as much.

PETER. Do you use powder or liquid?

SHANE. Um…

PETER. Powder is cheaper but liquid is better.

SHANE. Oh. Look, I just cleaned them in my sink but my room
    smells like damp, I think. I just used this soap stuff I bought.
    It's too chalky but.

PETER. Yeah, look, grab a bottle of liquid. Maybe you should go to a laundromat.

SHANE. I thought about that but how do you start? Do you just walk in with a bag of clothes?

PETER. Yes.

SHANE. Right.

PETER. It's fairly cheap.

SHANE. Is it? And like, you just go in? You don't ring them first or anything?

PETER. No.

SHANE. Cool. I might do that.

PETER. Are you fresh out of home?

SHANE. You can tell, hey. I don't fit in around here, hey. Everyone's a freak, hey. Not you. I didn't mean you're a freak.

PETER. That's okay.

SHANE. Yeah, you don't look like a Kings Cross person. Everyone around here looks like the guys who run dodgem cars at the show.

PETER. Oh they're all right.

SHANE. Carnies? No they're not. Only time people lock up their homes in Goulburn's when the show's in town.

PETER. Is that right?

SHANE. Yep. I reckon everyone locks their door all the time around here but. You must feel a bit, you know, living here, you must feel like, you're like surrounded by freaks. Do you?

PETER. Yes but I love it.

SHANE. I don't love it. I think it's friggin' ugly.

PETER. It just came back from the war a little bit mad. That's what I say. I've lived here for years and I love it. I walk home past the prostitutes and the bikies and the junkies and somehow I feel very at home.

SHANE. Yeah, you said that.

PETER. Am I repeating myself?

SHANE. Yeah but that's okay.

PETER. Must be time for another wine.

> PETER *pours another glass from a bottle of white wine in a cooler next to the table. He also has two cans of VB.*

Would you like one of these?

SHANE. I'm sweet.

PETER. No, go on. I can't work out happy hour to save my life. I asked for one wine and here I am with a bottle and two cans of VB. I can't drink all this myself.

SHANE. Really? Oh, okay but I'm a bit of a Cadbury. I might just take one home.

PETER. They're already open.

SHANE. Oh. Okay.

PETER. Happy times.

SHANE. Cheers.

> *They drink.*

PETER. Now I do like your hair.

SHANE. Oh nah. It was cheap. I think my hairdresser's a junkie.

PETER. I think it looks 'cool'.

SHANE. Thanks.

PETER. I'm Peter by the way.

SHANE. I'm Shane.

> SHANE *extends his hand to shake.*

PETER. How do you do, Shane?

SHANE. Good.

PETER. Gorgeous.

SHANE. Cool. Hey, look, Peter... I'm really sorry but I won't be able to shout you back a drink.

PETER. That's all right, mate.

SHANE. I would but I bought a toasted-sandwich maker yesterday and like –

PETER. Don't mention it.

SHANE. Cool. Just as long as you know.

PETER. Yes.

SHANE. Peter, you wouldn't be able to walk me home after this, could ya?

PETER. Oh, well...

SHANE. I just live like down there. I'm not like a drug user or anything.

PETER. I know.

SHANE. Cool. I'm not dodgy.

PETER. I know you're not.

SHANE. As long as you know that.

PETER. Drug-users don't have such beautiful skin.

SHANE. Oh no it's not.

PETER. It's so soft.

SHANE. I have heaps of pimples.

PETER. Where?

SHANE. Oh everywhere. In my T-zone.

PETER. What's your T-zone?

SHANE (*indicating a horizontal line above his eyes and a vertical one down the centre of his face*). It's here and here. It's my problem area.

PETER. Fuckin' pimples. Too funny. I'd trade a few things for pimples.

SHANE. And I noticed this the other day. If I squint. See?

PETER. What?

SHANE. Crows' nests or whatever.

PETER. Please.

SHANE. And my squint is lopsided.

PETER. Oh for goodness' sake.

SHANE. It's true. My face has changed.

PETER. I'm surprised they let you in here.

SHANE. Why? I'm nineteen. Do they ID here?

PETER. I've never been asked.

SHANE. But maybe they'll card me. I mean I am nineteen. I just left my licence in my flat. I'm on my blacks and everything.

PETER. Don't worry. You look nineteen.

SHANE. Do I?

PETER. Well sixteen at a push.

SHANE. Oh shit. Do you think so?

PETER. Drink up. It will be fine. I make you look older anyhow. No one too young would be drinking with this old thing. I might have to get you to walk me home. I left my walking frame by the Smokey Dawson chair so I'll need an arm to lean on.

SHANE. Do you have a walking frame?

PETER. No. I was joking.

SHANE. Oh right. I can walk you home if you want.

PETER. Oh Graeme'd love this. We'll see how we go.

SHANE. So how old are you?

PETER. Old enough. I don't do birthdays any more.

SHANE. Why not?

PETER. Because the last one was spent in a sauna.

SHANE. Why in a sauna?

PETER. Never mind.

SHANE. Hey, see that woman over there?

PETER. Where?

SHANE. Across the road.

PETER. Oh yes.

SHANE. I think she might be a prostitute.

PETER. Yes she is.

SHANE. Oh. Right. There you go, hey.

PETER. Why did you want me to walk you home, Shane?

SHANE. No reason.

PETER. Did you want me to see where you live?

SHANE. No.

PETER. I could come over if you want.

SHANE. Oh no, it's too messy for visitors. I just wanted someone to walk home with.

PETER. I understand.

SHANE. Yeah, I just get… You know.

PETER. What?

SHANE. I just get scared around here sometimes. I'm scared I'll get beaten up or something. I've heard of like gangs and stuff that smash people for fun. That happens in Sydney.

PETER. Not around here. They'd mug you for your phone here.

SHANE. Yeah, see? That's fucked. I don't have a phone but that's fucked. I'm scared of that. I'm getting streetwise but.

I never walk through parks and I walk in the middle of the
road so you can see people jumping out of bushes.

PETER. As long as you don't get hit by a car.

SHANE. That's better than being beaten up. At least in
Goulburn people punch your head in because they know you.
I hate Sydney sometimes.

PETER. It's actually fine. You don't have to be paranoid.

SHANE. Yeah, well, I've known violent people, like my
brother, he's full-on and I... Violent people scare me. And all
the junkies around here look like friggin' zombies and it's
fucked. I saw one fully bleeding from the head before
without knowing it. That's so fucked.

PETER. Well that's no good.

SHANE. And it's just tonight 'cause I didn't work today and
I just sat around by myself doin' bugger all. That's why I'm so
glad I met you because I reckon if I went another day not
talking to someone properly I'd fuckin' die. I was meant to see
this guy – this guy I served at the bottlo – but his phone
always goes to voicemail. I'm a bit weird in Sydney... I mean,
I'm just babbling on to you without letting you talk. I'd never
do that in Goulburn.

PETER. Well, I've never been to Goulburn.

SHANE. Oh, haven't ya? It's where that guy is.

PETER. Right.

SHANE. In the jail. The murderer. The famous one.

PETER. I don't know.

SHANE. I want to say Ivan Henjak but he used to play in the
Canberra Raiders and it's not him.

PETER. Right.

SHANE. Anyway, I'm from Goulburn too. I like to talk. Not
just think. You know how you see things – just little things –
that you would mention to another person. Like the shape

my sheets made the 'smorning looked like the map of
Australia. I had no one to tell that to, you know?

PETER. Where were the Snowy Mountains?

SHANE. What?

PETER. Nothing. You going to drink that or just hold it?

SHANE. Oh yeah. I don't drink beer much.

PETER. Have some wine.

SHANE. That's okay. You're actually not supposed to accept
drinks from strangers anyway.

PETER. Oh well, I'm okay.

SHANE. Yeah, I know. (*Drinks*.) Ivan Milat. That's his name.

PETER. The backpacker murderer?

SHANE. Yeah. He's in Goulburn. They have him in this room,
which is like suspended by chains and they have microphones
around it to listen for filing or digging. They reckon his only
motive is to get out now. That's all he thinks about.

PETER. Probably a few people who feel that way in Goulburn.

SHANE. Milat not Ivan Henjak. Do you like rugby league?

PETER. I buy the calendars.

SHANE. Oh right. Yeah, I don't like it any more. I don't know
what I like any more. Everything's changing.

PETER. You don't like eating alone.

SHANE. Nup.

PETER. But this isn't your meal is it?

SHANE. What?

PETER. The bar snacks.

SHANE. Oh. Yeah but I normally eat better.

PETER. Are you sure?

SHANE. Yeah. I had salad the other night. After I was coming back from this guy's house. The guy I met. The guy I served at the bottlo. Just this guy. I had this nice like pink salad from one of those shops on the main street bit here.

PETER. Like a seafood salad? I don't think they'd be very nourishing, young man. You'll have to come over for dinner.

SHANE. Really?

PETER. Yes. I'd love to cook for you.

SHANE. Cool. I'd love to let you.

PETER. Good. No I must because the last person I cooked for was my sister and it was simply hell, so no, I need to cook. What do you like to eat?

SHANE. I don't know.

PETER. I'd love to make a terrine. I read about terrines the other day. They're back.

SHANE. Cool. I don't know what that is.

PETER. It'll be a meat-cake thing. It's nice. Yes, I think I will do that.

SHANE. Cool. So why do you hate your sister?

PETER. Well, I don't hate her. I just think she's a bit of a pain in the arse. We've just been arranging some things and she's a moron. She can't help it.

SHANE. Is she the favourite? My brother was always the favourite.

PETER. Oh well, she probably was actually but my parents aren't around any more so it's not like that.

SHANE. Did they die?

PETER. Dad did. Mum's in a home now.

SHANE. Do you visit her much?

PETER. Well, she's in Adelaide. So it's pretty hard…

SHANE. Why?

PETER. She's completely dependent on nurses. She has to be lifted and washed. I'd be of no use to her. She's just not there any more.

SHANE. That's bad.

PETER. Have you ever been to a nursing home?

SHANE. No.

PETER. I've only been once – truth be known. Mum doesn't know because she doesn't know anything nowadays so... but I went in when she was first admitted... It smells like shit and there's all these desperate voices calling for nurses. Heavens above. And my sister was being all ridiculous and calling Mum 'dear' like she was the adult and Mum was a bloody toddler. And I saw the nurses lifting her onto this thing to be washed and I thought, hello, I can't do this. I just cannot do this.

SHANE. That must suck, hey.

PETER. But tell me about this boy you met.

SHANE. Oh, it sounds like I'm a poof or something?

PETER. Oh. Aren't you?

SHANE. Hey? Do you think I'm poofy?

PETER. Oh no. Not if you aren't. You were just going on about him and I thought you might be together but that's okay.

SHANE. Yeah, I'm not. It's just 'cause I'm in Sydney. It's made me a bit of a girl. I've been noticing my voice is higher. I can't explain it.

PETER. Probably just excitement.

SHANE. Yeah. So this guy...

PETER. Yes.

SHANE. Well, I met him. I served him at the bottlo. When you came in. He gave me the money. He and I, you know, hooked up. Yeah and he's really nice. We have heaps of fun. He says funny things. I want to think of something funny he said but I can't.

PETER. Sounds nice.

SHANE. It's okay to be gay here, hey?

PETER. Oh it's okay anywhere.

SHANE. Not in Goulburn. There wasn't one other gay person in Goulburn. Sorry, actually of course there was. Joel Cochrane was the only one... and me but I'm not gay. I'm not full-blown gay. I'm just... in Sydney. I reckon all the gay people from all the little towns come here.

PETER. Well, maybe. I escaped from Adelaide after all.

SHANE. Really? Are you gay?

PETER. Well. Yeah.

SHANE. Oh.

PETER. You don't have to sit further away.

SHANE. No I wasn't. I'm gay. I'm gay too.

PETER. Good.

SHANE. That's the first time I've said that.

PETER. Really?

SHANE. I've never said those words to anyone.

PETER. Feels good, doesn't it?

SHANE. Yeah. I mean, I'm probably bi.

PETER. Whatever, it doesn't matter.

SHANE. Yeah, I like girls and boys. Man, I know people who would smash me if they heard that.

PETER. Like who?

SHANE. Most people.

PETER. Your brother?

SHANE. Everyone.

PETER. Well, they're not here. Cheers.

SHANE. Cheers.

They drink.

Can I ask you something?

PETER. Yes.

SHANE. You know coathangers?

PETER. Yes.

SHANE. Where do you get them from?

PETER. I don't know.

SHANE. Yeah, there isn't a shop for them. Everyone just
    has them, hey. Especially the wire ones and they're the
    ones I want. I reckon if I hung my clothes they wouldn't
    smell damp.

PETER. I'm always throwing coathangers out. They must just
    grow. I'll give you some to start a crop.

SHANE. Oh. Okay. Thanks, Peter.

Pause.

So, how do you have anal sex? I tried the other night but it
    didn't work. It just didn't fit. I was able to do it to him but.

PETER. Oh…

***

SHANE's *bedroom in a boarding house. Some weeks later.*

SHANE *has opened the door to* WILL.

SHANE. Fuck! Hi.

WILL. Oh, hi, Shane.

SHANE. You scared me, hey. You knock really hard.

WILL. Sorry. How are you?

SHANE. Really good. Come in. This is cool. Jeez, it's been
ages. I'm so glad I finally got on to ya.

WILL. Yeah well I couldn't return your messages.

SHANE. Yeah, I know. I'm getting a phone soon. Sorry,
I probably left way too many messages on yours. I bet
I sounded dumber and dumber each time.

WILL. No. It's fine.

SHANE. So this is where I live. It's not like your place. Take
a seat.

WILL. Ta.

SHANE. I wish I had a chair to offer you.

WILL. No, that's fine.

WILL *sits on the bed.*

SHANE. Yeah, I'm probably going to get a chair… From
a second-hand place or something. I want like a nice wood
one. I might make one.

WILL. Cool.

SHANE. Hey, I was thinking about cooking some soup.

WILL. Where?

SHANE. There's a microwave under you there.

WILL. Oh.

SHANE. My friend gave it to me.

SHANE *retrieves a tin of soup.*

WILL. I won't eat. I thought we could go and get a coffee or
something. We could eat at a café or something if you want.

SHANE. Oh cool. Yeah, I never go to caffs or anything.
Let's hang out here for two more secs and then we'll go.
Is that good?

WILL. Yep.

SHANE. I haven't really had anyone over yet.

WILL. Haven't ya?

SHANE. Nah. Your pants are excellent.

WILL. They're new.

SHANE. Cool.

WILL. Yours are great too.

SHANE. No, these are old. They're too baggy. Baggy pants suck now. I want ones with zippers and all those pockets. Do you use that many pockets?

WILL. Nah.

SHANE. That's excellent.

WILL. Yeah.

SHANE. I'm close to the train station, hey.

WILL. Yeah. It's good.

SHANE. Yeah. What's that? Is that you knocking?

WILL. Yeah, I was just tapping my hand.

SHANE. Oh, that's okay. I thought it was something. Sometimes it creaks in here. I think it's haunted.

WILL (*referring to a light shining through the window*). Does that light keep you up?

SHANE. No. I'm going to get a blind but. People walking down those stairs can see right in. I'm scared they might break in if they saw my alarm clock or something. It's dangerous around here.

WILL. I've never had any trouble.

SHANE. I haven't either but I'm a bit 'you know' walking around. I think I'm going to buy a cricket bat. I saw a kid-sized one at one of them povo second-hand shops. 'Cause it is fully dodgy. A woman killed her baby with a hose at one of the houses near here.

WILL. How?

SHANE. Oh, in a bucket or something.

WILL. Shit.

SHANE. Yeah. A dancer from *Les Girls* was shot by a concreter and buried in the foundations of the Victoria Street apartments.

WILL. Fuck.

SHANE. Must have been drugs… Did you hear that creaking?

WILL. Nup.

SHANE. Yeah, it's a fuckin' ghost. If I see it I'm fuckin' leaving. I might do judo.

WILL. To take on a ghost?

SHANE. No, for self-defence. Get lessons. My brother used to do it. He was pretty good. He was in the paper heaps. And for swimming. He was good at stuff like that.

WILL. Right. Cool. So…

SHANE. Yeah?

WILL. How's the bottlo?

SHANE. Oh, good. You haven't come in as much as when I first met you.

WILL. Nup.

SHANE. I was a mong when I served you, hey.

WILL. No.

SHANE. Yeah, I stuffed it all up and they couldn't balance the till. They took me off register for a while. I'm back on it now.

WILL. So what else have you been up to?

SHANE. Nothing. Just hanging out. I see this friend, this old friend. We have dinner sometimes.

WILL. Cool.

SHANE. Are those bits in your hair fake?

WILL. The blonder bits are highlights.

SHANE. Awesome. Do you use gel?

WILL. Wax.

SHANE. I use gel but it goes too hard. See?

WILL. Yeah. It's really hard.

SHANE. I was trying to cover up the chunky bits from when
the hairdresser got the noddies. But this hair gel's too full-on
and it gave me a headache from the spiky bits when I sleep.
It's fully like glue and shit.

WILL. Yeah get a better one.

SHANE. Yeah. Can I feel your wax?

WILL. Um. Yeah.

SHANE. Cool. Sticky. Your hair's nice.

WILL. Thanks.

SHANE. You smell good too.

WILL. It's Issey Miyake.

SHANE. Cool.

    SHANE *leans in to kiss* WILL. WILL *pulls away.*

WILL. So when will you start judo?

SHANE. I don't know. I only just thought of it.

WILL (*karate-chopping* SHANE). Hee-ya.

SHANE. Piss off.

WILL. 'Abu-Kick'. Remember that? From *Mortal Kombat*.

SHANE. No, *Street Fighter II*.

WILL. Oh yeah.

SHANE. And it was 'Ryu-Ken'.

WILL. Was it? (*Playfully pushing* SHANE.) 'Ryu-Ken'.

They begin to wrestle and at some point they roll about on top of each other.

It wasn't 'Ryu-Ken'.

SHANE. Yes. Ryu and Ken were the ones who could use that move. You should do it with me.

WILL. Um. What?

SHANE. Judo.

WILL. Oh no. I don't need to.

SHANE (*tough*). Oh yeah?

They continue to play-fight.

WILL. You're dead, fucker.

SHANE (*tougher*). Oh yeah?

WILL *squeezes a pressure point on* SHANE.

Ow.

WILL. Oh, diddums.

WILL *squeezes a pressure point on* SHANE.

SHANE. Ow.

WILL. Pressure point.

WILL *squeezes a pressure point on* SHANE.

SHANE. Ow.

WILL. Another one.

WILL *squeezes a pressure point on* SHANE.

SHANE. Ow.

WILL. Pressure point. Ha ha.

SHANE *pinches* WILL.

Ow, don't pinch, girl. Pressure point.

WILL *squeezes a pressure point on* SHANE.

SHANE. Ow. (*Slapping* WILL.) Horsey-bite.

WILL. Don't spank, perv.

SHANE. How do you know where my pressure points are? My brother used to always do that. And this. (*Twisting* WILL*'s nipple.*) Now whistle. Whistle.

   WILL *whistles*.

WILL. What?

SHANE. No, it's meant to hurt so much that you can't whistle.

WILL. I like it but.

SHANE. Oh well, you wouldn't if my brother did it.

WILL. I might.

SHANE. Yuck. No, he's gross. What about dribble torture?

WILL. What's that?

SHANE. Oh it's fucked. He would hold me down like this.

   SHANE *pins* WILL *down*. WILL *lets him*.

WILL. Yeah?

SHANE. And then let spit dribble down and suck it up just before it hit my face… if I was lucky.

WILL. Yuck.

SHANE. Festy, hey.

   SHANE *looks as though he might spit*.

WILL. Don't do it.

SHANE. I won't. I'll just kiss you.

WILL. Okay.

   They pash heaps. They start feeling each other's bodies.

SHANE. We better, um. Sorry, frog in my throat. We better, um, go under the sheet if we're going to do this. People can see.

WILL. Oh.

SHANE *lifts the bedsheet over them, completely covering them. Their kisses grow in passion. They are feeling each other up.*

SHANE. It's a really dumb belt, I'm sorry. It's fully cowboy, hey.

WILL. You do it.

SHANE. I really liked it when you said 'Sit on my cock' at your place that time.

WILL. Cool.

SHANE. I'd never heard that saying before: 'Sit on my cock.'

WILL. Yeah.

SHANE. Yeah. It made me really horny.

WILL. Good.

SHANE. Sorry I didn't.

WILL. What?

SHANE. Sorry I didn't sit on your cock.

WILL. It's okay. Kiss me.

They kiss.

SHANE. That felt nice. I like kissing you.

WILL. Yeah.

They kiss again.

SHANE. Do you like it when I touch you there?

WILL. Let's just wank.

SHANE. You touch my balls.

WILL. Just wank.

SHANE. I liked it when you sat on my cock. I mean, that kind of didn't work, but when we changed positions and it did… that was so good.

WILL. Mmmm.

SHANE. One time you should root me. Do you like it?

WILL. Uh-ah.

WILL *interrupts* SHANE *with a pash.*

SHANE. Oh, you're such a good pasher. Do you want me to fuck you again?

WILL. No.

SHANE. Okay. Why won't you touch me more?

WILL *interrupts* SHANE *with a pash.*

Mmmh. I love…

WILL *interrupts* SHANE *with a pash.*

Ohh, do you want to cum soon?

WILL. Not yet.

SHANE. I love it when you just…

WILL *interrupts* SHANE *with a pash.*

Mmmh. I love it when you pash me suddenly like that.

WILL *interrupts* SHANE *with a pash.*

You're such a good kisser. My ex-best friend stayed at my house once and we woke up kissing in the middle of the night. It was so good.

WILL. Don't talk now.

SHANE. Cool. It's just you kiss like him…

WILL *interrupts* SHANE *with a pash.*

You're going to make me blow if you keep kissing me. I like your dick. I am going to blow soon. Do you want to blow?

WILL. Soon.

SHANE. Really soon?

WILL. No wait.

SHANE. I don't think I can.

WILL. Not yet.

SHANE. I'm trying.

WILL. Soon.

SHANE. Let's blow together.

WILL. Okay.

SHANE. Now?

WILL. Soon.

SHANE. Make yourself blow.

WILL. Okay.

SHANE. Okay?

WILL. Not yet.

SHANE. Now?

WILL. Soon. Soon.

SHANE. Better go now. 'Cause I can't wait now.

WILL. Okay.

SHANE. Yes?

WILL. Yes.

SHANE. Oh. Hang on. Yes?

WILL. Yes.

SHANE. Now!

WILL. Yes. Yes! Yes! Yes?

SHANE. I went. Far out, mine shot so far. Did you see it?

WILL. Kind of.

They take the sheet off.

SHANE. Mmh. I better take this to the laundromat.

WILL (*sighing*). Fuck. It is a bit echoey in here.

WILL *washes his hands in* SHANE*'s sink.*

SHANE. It's haunted. It's fucked. Sometimes it's fun to do it quick like that. We'll do it for longer next time but.

WILL. Yeah, no, it was good. I liked it.

SHANE. Me too. Even though we just wanked. Hey, you know how I don't have bum sex?

WILL. Yeah.

SHANE. It's not because I'm a virgin. I mean, I've got off with a boy, boys before, heaps and girls. I just haven't been fucked.

WILL. Oh no, that's fine. Don't worry about those things, Shane.

SHANE. Yeah. I had a boyfriend in Goulburn.

WILL. Cool.

SHANE. Yeah. Actually, he wasn't a boyfriend. He was my friend Joel.

WILL. Cool.

SHANE. Yeah but he's so immature.

WILL. Yeah, my ex sucks too.

SHANE. I bet you've had heaps of boyfriends.

WILL. Nah. Just one really.

SHANE. No way. You deserve more.

WILL. You're sweet.

SHANE. Sweet? You think I'm really young, hey.

WILL. No I don't.

SHANE. I'm nineteen. I just look young.

WILL. You're cute.

SHANE. Oh you think I'm so little and young.

WILL. I don't.

SHANE. You do so.

WILL. I think you're hot.

SHANE. I can't wait to fuck you again. That was so good. At your place. In the shower. I can do it for longer when we fuck.

WILL. Oh well, next time.

SHANE. So there'll be a next time?

WILL. Maybe. Why not?

SHANE. I haven't seen you for a while.

WILL. Yeah. I'm sorry about that.

SHANE. Were you avoiding me?

WILL. No.

SHANE. Sure?

WILL. Yeah.

SHANE. Cool. I hope not.

    SHANE *handles himself.*

    Sorry, just readjusting.

WILL. What?

SHANE. My balls.

WILL. Are they uncomfortable?

SHANE. I don't know.

WILL. Maybe I was kind of avoiding you but…

SHANE. Why?

WILL. …I have a good reason.

SHANE. I'm really needy, hey.

WILL. No. No. Nothing about you. Look, Shane, I think I could have given you something.

SHANE. What?

WILL. It's like warts.

SHANE. Warts?

WILL. It's a papilloma virus.

SHANE. Oh my God, what is it?

WILL. No, don't worry. Look, it's just this thing I have. I had. Not this time. Last time. I'm cured now. This is embarrassing. It's just this thing that grows like a rash and it can make you sick at first but it's basically just a –

SHANE. We used a condom, I can't catch AIDS, I hope you know.

WILL. No. It's nothing like that. It's really common.

SHANE. How did I get it? We used a condom.

WILL. Don't worry, man. It's easy enough to treat.

SHANE. What is it?

WILL. It's warts. It's like warts. I had it on my arse.

SHANE. Yuck.

WILL. Thanks.

SHANE. Yuck.

WILL. I didn't know I had it when we met. Anyway, the doctor was pretty relaxed about it. I think you have it on your balls. I have a brochure for you and a letter from the specialist to take to your GP.

   WILL *pulls out the brochure and note.*

SHANE. My GP's in Goulburn.

WILL. Just go to one here. Just take the note in.

SHANE. I can't afford it.

WILL. Doctors are on Medicare.

SHANE. I don't have a Medicare card.

WILL. Go and get one.

SHANE. Specialists aren't on Medicare.

WILL. You might not have to go to a specialist.

SHANE. I'll have to go back to Goulburn.

WILL. Just go soon. It's so so okay. It's just bad luck.

SHANE. Bad luck! Fuck you, giving me some fuckin' gay disease.

WILL. Shane. It's okay.

SHANE. No it's not. Dirty –

WILL. Shane, I'm sorry.

SHANE. Don't come near me, freak. You fuckin' freak.

WILL. Shane, come on. Don't be stupid.

SHANE. I'm not stupid. You're fucked. I got eighty for my UAI, you fuck… you pretty cock-sucking fuckin' slut. You're fuckin' disgusting. I can't fuckin' believe… Dirty fucking gay cunt.

WILL. Shane, calm down.

SHANE. No! Fuck you. Sydney's full of fucking…

WILL. I'm going.

SHANE. It's so fucking gross. Shit.

SHANE *cries*.

WILL. Hey, don't cry.

SHANE. Oh man…

WILL. Don't you have someone to talk to? A sister or something? Sisters are really good with this sort of stuff.

SHANE. I don't have one.

WILL. Your brother?

SHANE. This is so fucked for me.

WILL. It's really really nothing.

SHANE. It is for me. It so is for me.

WILL. Just go into any GP. I'll just leave the note here.

WILL *puts down the brochure and note.*

SHANE. Don't go, Will. Stay here tonight. I'm so excellent if you get to know me.

WILL *exits. A figure passes behind* SHANE.

Who the fuck is that?

SHANE *inspects the room. There is no one there.*

***

PETER*'s apartment in Elizabeth Bay. Several weeks later.* SHANE *is carrying an envelope.*

PETER. Hello, Shane. I wasn't expecting you until later. I've only just started marinating the meat.

SHANE. Oh yeah, I was just on my way to post a letter and thought I'd pop in to say hi. Glad you're here.

PETER. Are you okay? You've been crying.

SHANE. No I haven't.

PETER. You have. I can tell. Look at the red under your eyes.

SHANE. It's those itchy-ball trees near the station. They make me teary.

PETER. I hope everything's okay.

SHANE. Yeah.

PETER. Is it a love letter you're posting?

SHANE. No. Just to some people in Goulburn. You framed the terrine drawing.

PETER. Yes.

SHANE. It looks just like it. All the little meaty bits. It's really good, Peter.

PETER. Yeah, I'm not that happy.

SHANE. It must have taken ages.

PETER. No I just copied the photo out of the recipe book. Oh, the bloody cat still hasn't eaten her Whiskettes.

SHANE. Is she missing again?

PETER. No she finally came back but she's strange. I think she's found a tom. The slut. She was walking around here spraying her pheromones everywhere. I wish I could do that, just go into Midnight Shift and scent people.

SHANE. Yeah.

PETER. I just opened some Brie. Can I get you a wine?

SHANE. Bri? My brother's girlfriend's called Bri.

PETER. It's cheese.

SHANE. Nah, I'm right.

PETER. Is it that boy who made you cry?

SHANE. I haven't been crying.

PETER. You've been very hard to get out of the house lately.

SHANE. I was sick.

PETER. Lovesick, I bet.

SHANE. But I think it was just that seafood-salad stuff that I like.

PETER. Don't eat that stuff. But there's something else. With the boy.

SHANE. He's a cock. We had a fight.

PETER. When?

SHANE. Few weeks ago. He finally got my messages. He came over and he's so fucked.

PETER. Did he break it off?

SHANE. I wasn't going out with him. It wasn't a boyfriend thing. As if.

PETER. Oh well. Move on.

SHANE. Yeah. And um, I was thinking, I might need you to take me to…

PETER. Midnight Shift? No worries. I'll just grab my scent.

SHANE. You're funny.

PETER. Funnier than Will?

SHANE. No.

PETER. I hate him. I bet he's gorgeous.

SHANE. Whatever. Well, he is actually kind of hot. He has those lines.

PETER. What lines?

SHANE. Those Van Damme lines that angle towards his, you know…

PETER. His lunch.

SHANE. I couldn't send the letter that I was going to post. It was to home.

PETER. Don't get embarrassed and change the subject. I've told you about a lot of my roots over dinner and a glass or two. It's about your turn.

SHANE. Okay. But this isn't going into your wank bank is it?

PETER. Yes, a long-term deposit with a strong interest rate.

SHANE. Don't be gross. I'll only tell you because you're my friend and that's what best friends do. They sit around talking about, well, girls and boys.

PETER. I know.

SHANE. Yeah. He has a really smooth stomach. A six-pack.

PETER. Oh shit. Wait, start from the top.

SHANE. No. That's all. He sucks. With his stupid girl's hairdo and –

PETER. What colour?

SHANE. It has blond highlight bits.

PETER. Very gay.

SHANE. Yeah he's not like a pansy but. I wouldn't like that. I mean, his voice is a bit gay but not too gay.

PETER. Not like mine.

SHANE. Yours isn't too gay.

PETER. Oh good.

SHANE. His is like a normal boy's but also a bit gay so that it reminds you that you can have sex with him.

PETER. Yours is like that.

SHANE. Mine isn't gay at all.

PETER. Oh isn't it?

SHANE. No. Oh and, he so knows that his eyes are really good. He shows them off so much. Like just looks at you. He totally misled me.

PETER. Don't play dumb. It takes two to tango. What's his skin like?

SHANE. Oh it's soft. Like expensive soft. 'Cause I think he's rich. Like just spends money on stuff. So he smells nice too.

PETER. Like what?

SHANE. Is-he-markie.

PETER. Does he smell like fucking?

SHANE. What?

PETER. Sorry.

SHANE. I don't know.

PETER. Go on.

SHANE. With what?

PETER. Is he strong?

SHANE. Stronger than me. He's tall. Heaps taller than me. He must be six foot. He could pin me down.

PETER. Heavens.

SHANE. When he came to my house, we wrestled.

PETER. Wrestled?

SHANE. Yeah. That was my favourite bit. I felt like Mum was going to bust us for jumping on the bed or something but I didn't know he was a filthy fuckwit then.

PETER. Have you seen him with his shirt off?

SHANE. Yeah. At his house.

PETER. I love shirts coming off. It's always been my favourite bit.

SHANE. My favourite thing about him are his shoulders. He's huge. He's like a footy player. When he took his shirt off – his shoulders are like balls of muscle. And I like his lips. The line where it stops being lips and starts being face or the other way round is really, I don't know, like I made it up. It's like it's drawn.

PETER. And are his lips kissable?

SHANE. Yeah. And he's good at tonguing.

PETER. Oh really?

SHANE. Yeah.

PETER. I can imagine the shirt coming off.

SHANE. He has a little bit of soft hair in like a 'V' here – (*Indicating his upper chest.*) I think he clippers it but it's grown a bit so now it's soft. And he has a pretty hard chest. His nipples are low and brown and that's how I like them.

PETER. Me too. What's his body hair like?

SHANE. Um, it's kind of light brown. His tan has no gaps.

PETER. None?

SHANE. Nup. And yeah, he's hot.

PETER. Keep on going.

SHANE. With what?

PETER. You want to tell me about his cock.

SHANE. Okay, well, it's good. When I slipped his undies down he had a half-mongrel. It was just starting to move to one side and then up.

PETER. Goodness.

SHANE. I watched it grow. It's pretty big. It's thick.

PETER. Are you hard now?

SHANE. Yeah. A bit. My brother caught me with a boy once.

PETER. What else? Tell me more. Did the mongrel get 'full-on'?

SHANE. Are you?

PETER. What?

SHANE. Hard?

PETER. A bit. Are you more hard now?

SHANE. Yes. I want to be your friend.

PETER. Well, that's okay. Friends do this sort of thing all the time.

SHANE *undoes his belt. Silence.* PETER *gets on his knees before him.*

SHANE. My brother reckons faggots spread disease and they fuck kids and they're weak. Maybe that's true.

PETER. I'm sorry?

SHANE. I'm not like your other friends. I'm special.

PETER. All right, Shane. 'No' is fine. But don't carry on with bullshit. You know what's going on. You can't play the little kid for ever.

SHANE. But I am a kid.

PETER. Stop. Just stop it. It shits me. It really shits me when people your age pretend. The little country kid who has no idea will only go so far. For fuck's sake, switch on, Shane. Grow up and stop acting so fucking pathetic.

SHANE. I'm sixteen. I'm halfway through Year Ten.

PETER. But you said –

SHANE. I was lying.

PETER. Why?

SHANE. I ran away from home when my brother bashed the fuck out of me. You've done this before.

PETER. I beg your pardon.

SHANE. Yuck. Old sleaze.

PETER. Maybe you should go.

SHANE. You make me sick, ye dirty perv.

PETER. You're frightening me.

SHANE. Ye fuckin' cunt.

PETER. Just go, please. Get out.

***

SHANE *is in the laundromat. He takes a pile of linen and his laundry liquid from a sports bag.* BEN *enters.*

BEN. How are ya, little bro?

End of Act One.

ACT TWO

The laundromat. Continuing from the previous scene.

SHANE. Fuck. Don't come near me, Ben.

BEN. Fuckin' hell. I've driven halfway across the country, putting up signs and looking for you, Shane. Some cunt said you were in Byron. Mum and Dad are in fuckin' Mildura 'cause someone said you were picking fuckin' fruit and here you are in a fuckin' laundromat.

SHANE. Why did you come?

BEN. Because I wanted to find you. I've taken heaps of time off work.

SHANE. Don't come any closer.

BEN. This letter turned up.

SHANE. Beg ye pardon?

BEN. Been looking everywhere for you. Then the letter turned up.

SHANE. I never posted it.

BEN. It had a postmark on it so you must have.

SHANE. No I never. It's still up in my room.

BEN. It said Kings Cross post office.

SHANE. I don't think there is a Kings Cross post office.

BEN. There is.

SHANE. Is not. Don't come near me, Ben.

BEN. The bloke at the bottle shop said you'd be here. Cool place to work. Cases were expensive but. Posher than I thought around here.

SHANE. Are you drunk?

BEN. Too expensive.

SHANE. Toohey's Red's not expensive.

BEN. It's mid-strength.

SHANE. Toohey's Red's not mid-strength.

BEN. Yes it is.

SHANE. It's just on special.

BEN. Whatever. It's mid-strength.

SHANE. Whatever. It's not. I work there. I'd know.

BEN. Well, it is. You're wrong.

SHANE. You have to go.

BEN. So what's wrong with you? You sick?

SHANE. How'd you know that?

BEN. You are sick. Contagious?

SHANE. No. I'm not sick.

BEN. Said in your letter. What'd you need the Medicare
    number for?

SHANE. I don't. You're making it up.

BEN. Well, you can just get your own Medicare number so you
    fucked that up.

SHANE. I'm fine. There's nothing wrong with me.

BEN. Even Rocky misses you, hey.

SHANE. The fuckin' dog does not miss me.

BEN. She does. She's getting heaps fat now. Dad feeds her.
    He's been giving her two-minute noodles every night and
    Woollies' chickens on the weekends if they're reduced.
    Mum's stopped stopping him. It's comfort food because
    Rocky's missing you so much.

SHANE. Well, I don't believe that. I miss Rocky but. Did Dad want you to find me?

BEN. Yes.

SHANE. I bet Mum made youse.

BEN. No.

SHANE. I can tell you're lying. You and Dad hate me.

BEN. Shane, don't be a dick.

SHANE. Yeah, that's right. Criticise me all the time, why don't ya?

BEN. Don't be oversensitive.

SHANE. Oversensitive. Whatever, cockhead.

BEN. Shane, come on. Do you wanna go to Maccas and have a chat?

SHANE. To the café bit?

BEN. If you want?

SHANE. No. You wouldn't just come in here. You can't just come in here and pretend everything's okay, Ben.

BEN. You know practically the whole town's been trying to find you?

SHANE. Do they know what you did to me?

BEN. I don't know.

SHANE. Things get around. They should know.

BEN. Well...

SHANE. Fuckin' psycho. It's not my problem. And anyway, I don't think you are my brother no more.

BEN. I got punched in the head outside Pashes last week.

SHANE. That wasn't last week.

BEN. Still bruised.

SHANE. Where?

BEN. There.

But there's no bruise.

SHANE. Goulburn's got worse. It's got meaner.

BEN. Nah, it was one of my mates.

SHANE. Who?

BEN. Boxhead done it. He was pissed but and we're mates again now. See that's what blokes do. They forgive and –

SHANE. No, fuck off. Don't tell me what to do.

BEN. Shane, I'm going through a hard time, you know that. Think about stuff. And I broke up with Bri.

SHANE. When? Again?

BEN. I've been seeing this girl Terrine.

SHANE. As if.

BEN. Yeah I know. And she's a slut. I kind of hate her but I don't know. I just let things get to me sometimes and –

SHANE. Because you smoked too much pot.

BEN. No I don't.

SHANE. You had a billy every day for breakfast.

BEN. No, Shane, don't say shit about stuff you don't know about. Who said I had a billy for breakfast every day?

SHANE. You did. You told me that.

BEN. Pot just makes you forgetful; it doesn't do anything bad.

SHANE. It made you mean.

BEN. No it didn't. I don't smoke every day anyway. I don't smoke that much at all. You're full of shit, you are.

SHANE. Well something made you into a psycho.

BEN. No it didn't.

SHANE. Yes it did. I used to want to be like you when I grew up.

BEN. Err, whatever, fuck ya.

SHANE. I said not to come near me, Ben.

BEN. Are you going to come back home?

SHANE. No.

BEN. I got my hair cut. Do you like it?

SHANE. Kind of. I heard about Goulburn a few weeks back. About Reg.

BEN. Yeah, well...

SHANE. Are Mum and Dad still friends with him?

BEN. Yeah.

SHANE. But is he going to prison?

BEN. No. Newspaper's full of shit. I reckon we should go and get an ice block or something. It's hot. We could try to find Sunny Boys. Remember them?

SHANE. Nup.

BEN. Err, fuckin' dumb. Yes you do.

SHANE. No I don't.

BEN. Like a frozen popper. You do.

SHANE. I can't remember them.

BEN. Yes, you loved them. Sunny Boys.

SHANE. Maybe. They come in purple and orange?

BEN. Yeah, your favourite.

SHANE. I think I remember them. They weren't my favourite.

BEN. Yes they were. Let's go find them. I was thinking about them the other day.

SHANE. I don't think they make them any more.

BEN. They would.

SHANE. You reckon?

BEN. Yep, definitely.

SHANE. Well, I can't leave here and I don't want an ice block.

BEN. Why not?

SHANE. I'm waiting for my washing to finish and I've got stuff soaking in NapiSan.

BEN. I'll wait.

SHANE. No. I need to wash my stuff a few times and the water needs to be boiling, and it takes ages. So no.

BEN. Well, whatever. It is fuckin' hot.

SHANE. I've been listening to the news heaps. Is it true what Angela Bresnik is saying about what happened at the pool?

BEN. She's lying. She just wants to be on *A Current Affair*. Reg trained me the most, so I'd know. It's so dumb when newspapers say stuff like that. When I was a kid they said I was going to swim at the Olympics. Just because the newspaper says something. It actually means shit. Goulburn's shit. I've almost got my drainage apprenticeship.

SHANE. I know that. That was before.

BEN. Yeah. Only a few months to go.

SHANE. Then what?

BEN. I'll probably get heaps of work.

SHANE. That's good.

BEN. I'll get heaps of money. I could probably start my own business.

SHANE. How?

BEN. Get a loan. Interest rates are low. And just flog my boss's clients. He's a lazy rude fuck anyway so it wouldn't be wrong to take people away from him.

SHANE. That sounds good then.

BEN. I wanna get a new car too.

SHANE. Sell yours?

BEN. Yeah. Might sell it up here. Probably get more up here. Thought I might get you to help me. Where are you staying up here?

SHANE. I got a good place. I like it. I'm doing okay. It's got a fridge and everything.

BEN. Where is it?

SHANE. I'm not going to tell you, Ben.

BEN. Why not?

SHANE. I don't want you around me any more.

BEN. Well… No one would hurt you back in Goulburn, Shane. I'd protect you.

SHANE. What if I need protecting from you?

BEN. You reckon you're safe now?

SHANE. Hey?

BEN. Around here. A lot of weirdos.

SHANE. Oh, nah –

BEN. Shane, fuck, people are fucked up around here. There's like boy prostitutes and everything. That wall thing. Under the Coke sign.

SHANE. It's not under the Coke sign. It's the wall of the old jail.

BEN. Oh you know it, do you?

SHANE. No.

BEN. People might fuck you up, Shane. A homeless guy got scalped by vigilantes from Sutherland that want all the homeless people off the streets.

SHANE. I sleep with the radio on for security so I hear all the news. It seems dodgy around here but I've never had any trouble.

.

BEN. Well, still…

SHANE. I'm staying here.

BEN. How will you get by?

SHANE. I am getting by so that's okay, hey. Just let me finish my washing.

BEN. All right. So, I should go then. Goodbye, Shane.

> BEN *moves closer to* SHANE, *perhaps to hug him.*

SHANE. Don't touch me. Fuck off.

BEN. You've got to look after yourself. You're just little and young.

SHANE. I'll call the police.

BEN. They're targeting seat belts; I saw a sign.

SHANE. Just keep away.

BEN. I'll tell Mum and Dad you're okay.

SHANE. No. Just tell them I don't want anyone to come near me and I'm moving on anyway. They won't be able to find me.

BEN. Okay. Should we shake hands at least?

> *They shake hands.* BEN *doesn't let go.*

SHANE. See ya.

BEN. Shane… You could come back, you know?

SHANE. Let go of my hand.

BEN. Shane, come back.

SHANE. Let go of my hand.

BEN. You're excellent, Shane.

SHANE. Let go of my fuckin' hand, Ben.

BEN. I want to get to know you again.

SHANE. I said let go, cunt.

Whack! SHANE *hits* BEN *with the child-size cricket bat that he keeps in his laundry bag.*

I warned you. I warned you, Ben. Get out. I don't exist any more. Pretend you couldn't find me. I mean it. I never want to see you again.

BEN *stumbles back. The blow has sent him into a daze.*

***

WILL *emerges on the landing in front of his apartment.*
A month or two later.

SHANE. Hi, Will. It's me, Shane. You haven't forgotten me, have ya?

WILL. Just surprised to see you. What do you want?

SHANE. How are y'going?

WILL. Good. What d'ye want?

SHANE. So… Um… I was going to go play cricket. Can't play it on the road here. Play it in the park but. Wanna come? Cool shoes.

WILL. Look, I'm busy. I've got people inside.

SHANE. I got sacked from my job yesterday.

WILL. That's bad luck.

SHANE. Yeah. They're cunts.

WILL. I'm so not in the mood for this. Sorry.

SHANE. Tired?

WILL. Um… I've got family over and…

SHANE. Do you want me to come back later?

WILL. Not really.

SHANE. I can tell you want to get back inside.

WILL. That's right.

SHANE. Cool. Do they all live nearby?

WILL. Yeah. One's moving. It's a goodbye lunch. I have to go.

SHANE. Was there a falling-out?

WILL. No. She's just buying a house.

SHANE. I reckon your mum and dad would be cool.

WILL. Shane, I don't need this. And I'm coming down so it's not good timing.

SHANE. What do you mean, 'coming down'?

WILL. I took a pill last night so I'm feeling down.

SHANE. What kind of pill?

WILL. Ecstasy.

SHANE. Drugs?

WILL. Yeah.

SHANE. Why would you take something that makes you feel down?

WILL. It makes you feel good first.

SHANE. Keep your fluids up. Not too much but. That's how Sophie Delezio died. I think.

WILL. I think she's still alive.

SHANE. Is she? That's lucky.

WILL. So, um… I better go back inside. I'm watching *The Wiggles* with my nephew.

SHANE. They're creepy, hey.

WILL. Yeah. I like them today. Bye.

SHANE. I just came back because you make me horny. I wank about us.

WILL. I'm touched.

SHANE. You know how good your eyes are. I know you know. Do you want a head job?

WILL. Fuckin' hell. I'm fine, thanks.

SHANE. Like later. I could come back.

WILL. No thanks.

SHANE. I can tell you're a bit turned on by that.

WILL. No.

SHANE. Can I tell you something?

WILL. I've gotta go back inside.

SHANE. My favourite thing about you is your lips. They're so good. I reckon they look drawn on. I'll go. Can I just have one more kiss? Just one more kiss. I won't bother you any more. Cross my heart. Please.

WILL. I'm going.

SHANE. I'd love to meet your family.

WILL. Another time.

SHANE. Really?

WILL. Um. No.

SHANE. I wouldn't embarrass you in front of them. They wouldn't think I'm gay.

WILL. They wouldn't care about that.

SHANE. Do you introduce boys to them?

WILL. I could. But, um, there's nothing really between us, anyway, so…

SHANE. You wouldn't know anyone who could give me a job, would ya?

WILL. Nup.

SHANE. I'm going to get evicted if I don't pay my rent soon.

WILL. You're not having a good time.

SHANE. Do you know how to get on the dole? I could get it, hey.

WILL. Yeah. Guess so.

SHANE. It's Centrelink, hey.

WILL. Yeah.

SHANE. Would I need papers and stuff?

WILL. They'll be able to tell you.

SHANE. I couldn't use your phone, could I?

WILL. Couldn't you just use a public phone?

SHANE. Yeah. Sure. So um… you did give me those warts.

WILL. Sorry.

SHANE. They got really bad.

WILL. Sorry.

SHANE. Which doctor did you go to? I want a good one.

WILL. Haven't you been yet?

SHANE. Not yet. Do you have another one of those letters? I threw it out.

WILL. You probably should go pretty soon.

SHANE. Yeah. You're telling me. They've got pretty bad.

WILL. How bad?

SHANE. Infected, I think. Festy. Colourful.

WILL. Fuckin' hell. Shit. You gotta look after yourself, dude.

SHANE. I was scared to go in by myself.

WILL. Why?

SHANE. Could you come in with me?

WILL. I don't think I need to.

SHANE. Do you know that I'm younger than you think?

WILL. What do you mean?

SHANE. I'm in Year Ten.

WILL. Fuck. Where?

SHANE. Nowhere now.

WILL. Right.

SHANE. I'm sixteen so…

WILL. Well, Shane, um… Call me, if… I mean, I don't know what I can do for you.

SHANE. I know we're not going to…

WILL. Yeah, we're not. Don't put any expectations on me but… If you really need someone to… I don't know. Just look after yourself. Go see a doctor. Today.

SHANE. Yeah.

WILL. Promise?

SHANE. Yeah.

WILL. And um…

WILL reaches into his wallet and pulls out a fifty-dollar note.

You've got other friends. Don't you?

SHANE. Yep. Another friend.

WILL. Good.

WILL gives SHANE a peck on the cheek.

Take this too.

WILL hands SHANE the money.

SHANE. Oh ye sure?

WILL. Yeah. It's fine.

SHANE. Thanks, mate.

WILL. See ya.

They shake hands.

SHANE. You're excellent, Will.

SHANE *releases* WILL*'s hand.*

WILL. Bye.

WILL *exits.*

***

PETER*'s door.*

PETER *is wearing a rather feminine kitchen apron.*

PETER. Mmm. What have we got here?

SHANE. I was just nearby and thought I'd knock.

PETER. Did you?

SHANE. Thought I'd say g'day. See how you're going.

PETER. Fine.

SHANE. That's good. I was hoping I'd just run into you but I'm not working at the bottlo any more.

PETER. You puzzle me, Shane.

SHANE. Can I come in?

PETER. Shane, some things were said…

SHANE. Sometimes mates fight.

PETER. What do you want, Shane?

SHANE. Just thought I'd see how you are. Did your cat come back?

PETER. No. They go away to die.

SHANE. Poor cat.

PETER. Just a cat. I'm not some lonely old poof with a cat, am I?

SHANE. No.

PETER. No. I've got my pot plants now.

SHANE. Oh good.

PETER. It was good to catch up with you, Shane.

SHANE. Oh. Do you wanna go have a coffee or something?

PETER. Bit busy actually. And look, Shane. I don't like it when you claim, like Graeme claims, like everyone thinks, that just because an older man takes an interest that he's thinking with his dick. It wasn't like that. I enjoyed your company. That's all.

SHANE. I'm weird. I've gone weird, Peter. I talk to myself. I've gone fucked in the head. I don't know what I'm saying sometimes.

PETER. Was it true? What you told me?

SHANE. What?

PETER. About you? About your brother?

SHANE. Yes. Promise it is. They couldn't get him off me. It was bad. He broke the bit of bone in my cheek that's like a tabletop. It was completely crushed. He was like a bull terrier. He even growled. It was so fucked. I'm not making it up. I just can't work out why he went psycho.

PETER. You must hate him.

SHANE. No. No I don't. I've been trying to pluck up the courage to go home but I can't. There's no way I can go back and I… I have to go to hospital, hey.

PETER. What for?

SHANE. It doesn't matter.

PETER. What? It does matter. Tell me.

SHANE. I have an STD.

PETER. What is it?

SHANE. It's a bad one.

PETER. Oh… What?

SHANE. Warts.

PETER. Warts! Oh no, that's fine. Bit of nitrogen or whatever. They freeze them off. Watch them though because you can have a recurrence. I had them once and it took five goes to get rid of them. Either that or I had warty trade five nights in a row and one mustn't discount that possibility.

SHANE. Mine's past that. It's on my arse and my balls. All across my Mars bar. I left it.

PETER. What's a Mars bar?

SHANE. It's the bridge bit from your balls to your arse.

PETER. Oh. I'm going to use that.

SHANE. I should have gone to the doctor. I just couldn't work out how. At home I would have just asked my mum to take me. But anyway I went and it was awful. The doctor said 'Why didn't you come to see me earlier? Were you hoping to grow a beanbag on your arse?'

PETER. What a hoot.

SHANE. And I just cried. I don't want to be a freak. I didn't know they would get this bad. I thought they would just go away.

PETER. You could have come and told me that. I used to get STDs. I remember my first one. I thought Satan was forcing himself out of my penis. I was a Christian then. Don't ask. But I found out I had the clap and they just give you a jab and it goes. Of course, some things aren't that easy to get rid of and, of course, they're all serious.

SHANE. I wore a condom.

PETER. Yes, you can still get stuff though. They say to even wear a condom for head now but, I mean really, you might as well stay at home and suck on a dildo.

SHANE. Yeah, well, I haven't had sex for ages.

PETER. Oh, you poor thing. Join the club. I'm on the ladies' auxiliary. So what happens now?

SHANE. I have to go to hospital they're so bad.

PETER. When do you go in?

SHANE. I'm waiting for a place. It'll be day surgery.

PETER. Oh well that'll be fine.

SHANE. They put me out and everything and, well, I have to have someone to collect me. They said I have to have someone.

PETER. I'll do it.

SHANE. Will you? It might be a weekday.

PETER. I'll take the day off.

SHANE. I'll pay for the cab.

PETER. No you won't.

SHANE. You won't have to take the whole day off. You just need to be there to 'escort me home' in case I'm too spasticated from the drugs.

PETER. I'll take the day off and I'll sit and wait for you. We'll go together in the morning. It will be 'awesome'.

SHANE. I'll wake up as soon as I can.

PETER. It'll be fine, Shane.

SHANE. I know you said you hate hospitals because of your mum.

PETER. Did I say that?

SHANE. Yeah, you hate the smell.

PETER. Oh well, no but that's true enough. But this sounds like the perfect excuse for the day off work.

SHANE. I didn't have anyone to ask. When they said I had to have someone I said, 'What if I have no one?' and they said I must have someone.

PETER. And they were right.

SHANE. I don't like hospitals.

PETER. Have your family contacted you?

SHANE. Not a peep. They don't care and I can't go back.

PETER. Are you hungry? I could make you something. A piece of sticky date pudding?

SHANE. Okay.

PETER. It was a joke.

SHANE. Oh. Shut up.

PETER. Come in. Make yourself comfortable. Wish I had a beanbag to offer you.

SHANE. I said shut up.

***

SHANE*'s place.*

SHANE *has a half-packed travel bag and some stuff to make a sandwich. His arse and balls are itchy.* BEN *enters.*

SHANE. Fuck. No way. Please don't hurt me, Ben. I'm sorry.

BEN. I'm not here for trouble. I thought we could go for a swim. Have you got togs?

SHANE. How'd you… My door was locked.

BEN. It wasn't.

SHANE. It always is.

SHANE *retrieves his cricket bat.*

BEN. You can hit me again if you want.

SHANE. I might.

BEN. If it makes you feel better.

SHANE. You've gone weird. Who told you I lived here? Those bottle-shop cunts. I didn't take any money. They're fucked. Did they see one of your signs? I've never seen one. I've been looking for them. Where do you put them up?

BEN. I need to talk. I just need to talk. Please. I'm your brother. Can't you trust me? I promise I won't hurt you. Put the bat down, mate.

SHANE. No. Why can't you disappear out of my life?

BEN. I've tried. But it won't work. Come back. Mum's waiting for you to come back. You should see her hair but. She came home from the hairdresser and it was so big and curly. It was like she'd gone in and asked to look like Barnsie in Chisel. Fuck Dad and me laughed. Couldn't help it. I was ripped so I couldn't stop. Mum cried and I got paranoid but then she laughed and it was okay. We don't laugh much no more. She can't sleep. She has nightmares. A pipe bust open on me the other day. Shit poured on me and everything. I didn't snap. I'm not going to get into fights no more. There's heaps of Lebs in Goulburn. They're moving there from Sydney. It's dangerous. They fight in packs. It was hot as all fuck on the road. Was worried my new tyres would melt. Nan might not move down the coast no more. There are Lebs there too. And junkies. Terrorist junkie Lebs everywhere and the drought. Council's got to do something. More roundabouts. Ivan Milat's running for mayor but.

SHANE. You're not making sense.

BEN. It's such a hot day. Come back. We'd drive straight to the pool. Straight down the highway. Straight through town. Straight to the pool. Dive in and swim to the other side.

SHANE. You just want to beat me in a race.

BEN. I'd let you win.

SHANE. Are Mum's nightmares about me?

BEN. You could come back because it's not your fault.

SHANE. You're not yourself.

BEN. I hurt you. I remembered your face. I remembered seeing your face. I saw it in my sleep. All the time. I reckon you see it in yours.

SHANE. I'm scared of you.

BEN. You looked so shocked. I don't know what made you look like that. I hurt you. But I don't think it was my fault. I wasn't me. It wasn't me hurting you. I was someone else. It wasn't anything to do with you.

SHANE. Ben, I've never seen you like this.

BEN. I've always been like this inside.

SHANE. I never sent that letter, Ben.

SHANE *has the letter.*

BEN. I miss you, Shane. Don't move further away.

SHANE. Some things can't be undone, Ben.

BEN. Maybe I want to hurt myself, Shane, not you.

SHANE. Why?

BEN. I want you to be the one to find my letter.

SHANE. Don't do that.

BEN. Then come back. It's such a hot day. I haven't been to the pool for ages.

SHANE. Are you okay now, Ben?

BEN. I don't know. I feel strange.

SHANE. It's like you're coming down.

BEN. I'm not a druggo, Shane. You think I am.

SHANE. No I don't. Maybe I can make you a sandwich. I'm making a sandwich to give to my friend. I have really nice bread and stuff. I was going to make him a really full-on one. I could make you one too.

BEN. What's going on, Shane?

SHANE. Come and help me make a sandwich. Would you like that?

BEN. Yeah.

SHANE. I've got chicken luncheon. You like that, hey.

BEN. Chicken loaf?

SHANE. Chicken loaf. I knew there was another name for it. It says 'chicken luncheon' on the packet. I knew we called it something different. I couldn't remember. Chicken loaf.

BEN. 'Pressed chicken'. Some people say that. Not us but.

SHANE. I have devon too.

BEN. I hate that.

SHANE. I love it. I got this kind of lettuce. It's called 'rocket' which is cool.

BEN. Yeah, I've had that. It's spicy lettuce.

SHANE. Is it?

BEN. Yeah.

SHANE *makes two sandwiches as he talks.*

SHANE. Cool. I got mustard. I spent heaps. But I wanted it to be a good sandwich.

BEN. Yeah. I should bring you up some of Mum's relish.

SHANE. Nah, I've always hated Mum's relish.

BEN. No, Shane, it's an acquired taste. That's what she says and she's right.

SHANE. Maybe.

BEN. It's true.

SHANE. I have cordial as well. Do you like fruit-cup cordial?

BEN. I love it. You know that.

SHANE. Okay then.

SHANE *prepares a cup of cordial for* BEN.

BEN. Fuck, it's a hot day. Wish I could just go for a swim.

SHANE. I'm going to make the cordial really strong.

BEN. Good. Remember how Reg used to say there was a chemical that would make your wee go fluoro-pink?

SHANE. Yeah.

BEN. I believed that. I still haven't ever pissed in a pool since. Funny, hey. I guess there could be a chemical for that but it probably is bullshit, hey.

SHANE. Yeah. I always thought Reg was a mean cunt.

BEN. Yeah. I think maybe he was. I used to love the pool but. Remember we used to kick up such a fuckin' stink when we'd wake up so early on a Saturday and have to go. And Dad'd threaten us with the strap. You'd hate getting there but once you were, you wouldn't want to get out. I loved the pool. Do you reckon someone would have punched Reg's head in in prison yet?

SHANE. Probably. Is he in Goulburn, is he?

BEN. Yeah. It's too close but. I agree with the paper. They should have put him in another maximum security.

SHANE. Are you squares or triangles?

BEN. Squares.

SHANE. I'm triangles.

SHANE *cuts the sandwiches and hands* BEN*'s over.*

BEN. Thanks, mate.

SHANE. I heard something about Reg's lawyer getting him isolated.

BEN. That's fucked but. That's the reason people go to prison. Otherwise just put him in the Olympia Motel or something. Fuck him. He wrecked people's lives. Strong cordial.

SHANE. Yeah. Do Joanne and Kyle still live in town?

BEN. They had to move away.

SHANE. Poor cunts.

BEN. Yeah, poor cunts. He never touched his own kids but.

SHANE. Did he ever touch you?

BEN *eats his sandwich in silence*. SHANE *doesn't eat his*.

BEN. Yes.

SHANE. Did I see?

BEN. No.

SHANE. You remembered seeing my face. I looked shocked. Was it there? Was I little?

BEN. It's a hot day today.

SHANE. Where did you see my face?

BEN. I don't know where. I didn't know what was happening. We could try to find Sunny Boys.

SHANE. What did I see?

BEN. I don't know. I don't know if he made you or if you were just there. I hope he didn't make you. But it only happened one time of heaps of times. You saw.

SHANE. Was it at the pool?

BEN. Me just standing there letting him because I was his best swimmer. You saw. You saw all that. You must have forgotten.

SHANE. That's what was happening.

BEN. It's true. You saw. You saw me with a stiffy too. He used to give me a stiffy. And you saw. Is that what made you into a 'you-know'?

SHANE. No. That's not... No one could think that.

BEN. They could. You saw. You left. Mum and Dad couldn't protect me either. As if I'd cry, Shane. You're just making that up. I never cry.

BEN *wipes away a tear.*

You can't go back because I'll beat the fuck out of you. No one will be able to stop me.

SHANE. You can't hurt me any more, Ben.

BEN. When I saw you with that little kid in your room. You're fuckin' disgusting. I can't fuckin' believe –

SHANE. Little kid? That was Joel. He's fifteen.

BEN. Don't come near me, freak. You fuckin' freak.

SHANE. He's not a little kid. He just looks young.

BEN. He hasn't developed yet. You're like Reg.

SHANE. Is that what you think? He's fifteen. You know that. He was in my class. It's not like I'm old. You just don't get it. You're scared. We were just... I loved Joel. And I... I don't want you to hurt yourself.

BEN *eats in silence.*

I wish you would come to the Cross and put up signs.

BEN *finishes his sandwich and picks some crumbs off the plate.*

I don't have anyone. No one knows me here, Ben. I'm really alone. Come find me.

PETER *knocks.*

PETER. Knock knock.

SHANE. Hi, Peter. Come in.

PETER. The door's locked.

SHANE. Oh sorry.

SHANE *opens the door for* PETER. BEN *is invisible to* PETER.

PETER. Dear, it's a warm morning. I think it's going to be a stinker.

SHANE *wraps his sandwich in Glad Wrap to give it to* PETER.

Have you packed some stuff?

SHANE. Yeah and I made you a sandwich – to have for lunch at the hospital.

PETER. Oh darling, you gem. I'm touched.

SHANE *puts* BEN*'s plate away.*

SHANE. Don't know why I got this plate out. I can't eat before the operation.

PETER. No, oh well. I'm making us something nice tonight.

SHANE. Cool.

PETER. Well, got everything?

SHANE. Think so.

PETER. Good. Okay then. Cab's outside.

PETER *exits.*

***

PETER*'s bathroom. Later that day.*

SHANE *sees that* WILL *is present.*

WILL. He's all right, hey?

SHANE. Who?

WILL. Your friend. Peter.

SHANE. Yeah, Will, Peter's heaps good.

WILL. He likes to cook.

SHANE. Yeah.

SHANE *notices* WILL *is holding a towel.*

Are we going for a swim?

WILL. No, you're having a bath. He just asked me to grab you a towel.

SHANE. Oh yeah. Thanks for letting me recover here. Your place is better.

WILL. This is Peter's place. Fuck, you're out of it.

SHANE. No. I'm cool.

PETER enters. He runs the bath.

PETER. I hope you'll be okay in here. You've got a towel. I only cleaned in here yesterday. I hope there's enough hot water. There should be.

WILL. This one's all over the place, Peter. You might want to keep an eye on him.

PETER. Who made me matron?

WILL. I'm the guest.

PETER. Do you feel okay?

SHANE. Yeah, it's just a bit hazy.

He looks to WILL.

I feel nice but.

PETER. You're on happy pills, darling.

SHANE. My arse hurts but, hey. Did you get the salt?

PETER. Oh yes. I popped down when you were under the knife or above the surgeon or whatever they did to you.

WILL has found the salt.

WILL. There you are.

SHANE. How much do you use?

WILL. Heaps.

WILL punctures the bag and pours it in.

SHANE. Is it expensive?

PETER. Seventy-four cents a bag.

SHANE. I'll pay you back.

PETER. No you won't.

SHANE gets a bit light-headed as he leans over the bath.

You right?

SHANE. Yeah. Is Will staying?

PETER. I think so. He likes my apricot chicken too much.

SHANE. It's nice you came, Will. (*To* PETER.) We're not
boyfriends but. We just wrestle on the couch sometimes.
(*To* WILL.) It's okay that we're not boyfriends.

PETER. It's a big city.

SHANE. Yeah. Sorry I didn't finish your dinner. It was nice.
I just felt like spewing.

PETER. Oh, thanks. It'll keep.

SHANE. I should have known I was allergic to the penicillin.
See Mum knows those things. Not me.

SHANE *pulls off his top. It gets a bit caught on his head
and* PETER *helps him.*

I hope I'm not allergic to anything else.

PETER *moves to exit.*

PETER. I could ring your mum.

SHANE. No.

PETER. Not to tell her about anything, just to check that you
aren't allergic to anything else.

SHANE. She would think I was sick or hurt or something if you
asked about that.

WILL. Maybe she would want to know that you're not.

PETER *gets a glass of water.*

PETER. I'll just pop that down there for you.

SHANE *leans over to test the water again. It hurts.*

SHANE. Fuck, I'm like an old man or something.

WILL. Want some help?

SHANE. I'll be all right.

PETER. All right. We'll leave you to it.

> PETER *and* WILL *go to leave.*

SHANE. Could you stay?

PETER. Sure.

> PETER *is careful to respect* SHANE*'s privacy.*

SHANE. I won't be long. It will help me relax.

PETER. You'll feel better soon.

> SHANE *undresses. He has brown antiseptic around his shaved genitals.*

WILL. You right?

> *They help him into the bath.* SHANE *settles.*

SHANE. They shaved my nuts.

WILL. Did they?

SHANE. Yeah.

WILL. It'll grow back quick.

SHANE. The bath makes me feel better.

PETER. Good. I'll put your dinner in a Tupperware container if you want.

SHANE. Okay. It was really nice.

PETER. It was one of Mum's recipes. She sent it to me years ago but I'd never made it. I found it the other day. It just fell out of the bottom drawer in the kitchen. About an hour before the phone call came through. Funny how things happen.

SHANE. When's the funeral?

PETER. Next Tuesday. I'm not going. It'll be too...

SHANE. You should. I'll go with you.

PETER. No, you can't afford that and...

SHANE. I want to. If it will help you.

PETER. It… The plane trip home alone's what I'm dreading.

SHANE. Okay. Book us both a seat.

PETER. Okay.

SHANE. I'll pay you back.

PETER. No need.

SHANE. Maybe I could call my mum. I miss her.

PETER. You could call her from here later.

SHANE. I won't tell her about this.

PETER. No.

SHANE. I'm scared my dad would answer.

WILL. They must be worried about you.

SHANE. Imagine if my brother answered.

WILL. That'd be good.

SHANE. No, he's not like you, Will.

PETER. You do what's best.

SHANE. Do you miss your mum?

PETER. I'm sad it couldn't have been better. I should have cared for her. That's the deal: they care for us when we're young and we care for them when they're old. No matter what happens in between, that's the deal. I didn't come through on my end of the bargain.

SHANE. I could call them and say I'm okay. I want to go back to school.

PETER. I'm glad.

SHANE. I wanna finish. Not there but. I can't. Here. I could find somewhere here. Maybe my mum would send me money.

PETER. We could work that out.

SHANE. I could do that. I could ring them later. Might be good if Ben answered. I might just go, 'I love you.' Wonder what he'd say to that. Could you please pass us the water?

PETER. Sure.

SHANE (*taking the glass*). Thanks, Peter.

PETER. Good, Shane.

SHANE *drinks the water.*

The End.

A Nick Hern Book

Strangers in Between first published in Great Britain in 2016 as a paperback original by Nick Hern Books Limited, The Glasshouse, 49a Goldhawk Road, London W12 8QP, by arrangement with Currency Press Pty Ltd, PO Box 2287, Strawberry Hills, NSW 2012, Australia, www.currency.com.au

Strangers in Between copyright © 2006, 2016 Tommy Murphy

Tommy Murphy has asserted his right to be identified as the author of this work

Designed and typeset by Nick Hern Books, London
Printed in the UK by Mimeo Ltd, Huntingdon, Cambridgeshire PE29 6XX

A CIP catalogue record for this book is available from the British Library

ISBN 978 1 84842 585 9

Other Titles in this Series